# THE EVERYTHING KIDS' ENViRONMENT BOOK

**Learn how you can help save the environment—
by getting involved at school, at home, or at play**

Sheri Amsel

Foreword by Christopher J. Maron, Champlain Valley Program
Director, The Nature Conservancy, Adirondack (NY) Chapter

**adams**media
Avon, MA

**EDITORIAL**

Innovation Director: Paula Munier
Editorial Director: Laura M. Daly
Associate Copy Chief: Sheila Zwiebel
Acquisitions Editor: Kerry Smith
Development Editor: Brett Palana-Shanahan
Production Editor: Casey Ebert

**PRODUCTION**

Director of Manufacturing: Susan Beale
Production Project Manager: Michelle Roy Kelly
Prepress: Erick DaCosta, Matt LeBlanc
Interior Layout: Heather Barrett,
Brewster Brownville, Colleen Cunningham,
Jennifer Oliveira

An Everything® Series Book.
Everything® and everything.com® are registered trademarks of F+W Publications, Inc.

Published by Adams Media, an F+W Publications Company
57 Littlefield Street, Avon, MA 02322. U.S.A.
*www.adamsmedia.com*

ISBN 10: 1-59869-670-X
ISBN 13: 978-1-59869-670-7

Printed in the United States of America.

The pages of this book are printed on 100% post-consumer recycled paper.

J   I   H   G   F   E   D   C

**Library of Congress Cataloging-in-Publication Data**
available from publisher

This publication is designed to provide accurate and authoritative information with regard to the subject
matter covered. It is sold with the understanding that the publisher is not engaged in rendering legal,
accounting, or other professional advice. If legal advice or other expert assistance is required, the ser-
vices of a competent professional person should be sought.

    —From a *Declaration of Principles* jointly adopted by a Committee of the
American Bar Association and a Committee of Publishers and Associations

Many of the designations used by manufacturers and sellers to distinguish their products are claimed as
trademarks. When those designations appear in this book and Adams Media was aware of a trademark
claim, the designations have been printed with initial capital letters.

Cover illustrations by Dana Regan.
Interior illustrations by Kurt Dolber.
Puzzles by Beth L. Blair.

*This book is available at quantity discounts for bulk purchases.*
*For information, please call 1-800-289-0963.*

See the entire Everything® series at *www.everything.com*.

# Dear Parents,

It's no secret that kids love to help out. Participation builds their self-confidence and it helps them to feel connected to the community. Using this book, you and your child can discover lots of fun ways to get involved and protect the environment. Along the way, you'll help them understand how the earth works.

With *The Everything® Kids' Environment Book*, your kids will learn about:
- How the atmosphere and ozone layer protect us from the sun's rays
- Animals who live in the rainforest, wetlands, polar regions, and deserts
- The effects of noise pollution and why trees are important
- What the "greenhouse effect" is and how acid rain affects the air and temperature
- Which animals are extinct and how you can help protect others
- How recycling and composting work—and the benefits of both
- Organic foods and how they are produced
- How wind and solar power can light up and heat your home

Together, you and your kids can start protecting the environment today with these fun, step-by-step activities:
- Make your own cool art paper using recycled paper grocery bags
- Organize a cleanup effort in your local park or playground
- Host a bake sale to raise money for environmental efforts
- Learn about environmentalists and what they do to help
- Participate in Earth Day celebrations
- Plant a tree or start a garden

Get ready to go on an adventure with your children—one in which you'll unlock the magic of the environment and discover what you can do—together—to help keep the earth healthy for another 4.5 billion years!

# Contents

## DEDICATION

For Richard, who plants trees.

## ACKNOWLEDGMENTS

I would like to acknowledge the generous assistance of Dr. Stephen Carleton at SUNY Downstate Medical Center for his insights and online research assistance.

# Foreword

We all want our children to learn about the environment, value its fascinating interconnectedness, and make choices that preserve our world. We take our kids on nature hikes, walk through parks with them, and answer endless questions like "What is in a cloud?" In *The Everything®
Kids' Environment Book*, your child will get a complete introduction to the earth's habitats, biological treasures, and ecological processes. Then, after learning about threats to the environment, your child can see ways to help preserve this wonderful world we call "home."

Throughout the book, author Sheri Amsel provides fun and easy experiments you can do at home with your child to help provide answers to their questions. Instead of going through a lengthy and confusing parental explanation, Sheri says to use an empty plastic bottle, some warm tap water, and a match, then follow a two-step instruction and presto—you have a cloud in a bottle. The text in this book will provide explanations of this and other experiments your kids will enjoy doing—and they will learn while having fun.

If you are like me and you want your children to know about science, you reach for books like *Physics in the Bathtub* and *Science Experiments for Rainy Days*. These books have been useful and yet there are very few, if any, children's books that successfully take on the topic of the environment. As a conservationist, I have been looking for a book like *The Everything® Kids' Environment Book* to complement the lessons we learn outside.

I first encountered Ms. Amsel's writing and artistic expertise in a book called *A Wetland Walk*, which was our son's favorite book for about two years. In it, he learned about the beauty and mysteries of wetlands through her gentle words; he saw himself in her pictures, peering through the cattails to catch glimpses of dragonflies and frogs. Now, in *The Everything® Kids' Environment Book*, our son can go beyond wetlands to the larger world to see how humans affect the planet, and adopt the type of environmental ethics that will always be with him.

This book takes on one of today's greatest challenges—the environmental education of our children. This is an especially important task because kids should be exploring the outdoors as much as we did. The lessons and hands-on experiments will grab their attention and increase their understanding of the world, how it works, and how they can help protect it. Books like this are sure to inspire them to be outside in nature more often and to test their indoor experiments in the real world. And through this process, our children will become better citizens—ones who can probably teach us a thing or two about our "home," the earth.

   —Christopher J. Maron, Champlain Valley Program Director
   The Nature Conservancy—Adirondack (NY) Chapter

# Introduction

When people hear the word *environment*, they often think it has something to do with the people that protect the earth, but in truth the word *environment* is a scientific term. It means "all the living and nonliving things on Earth." The living things include animals, plants, bacteria, algae, fungi, etc. The nonliving things include rocks, mountains, streams, lakes, rain, snow, and even clouds, oxygen, and carbon dioxide.

The earth has many cycles that keep it in balance. Everything is interconnected and affects everything else, in ways we may not even realize. The water cycle keeps moisture falling as rain and snow and evaporating back up to the clouds to fall again. The oxygen cycle depends on plants replenishing the oxygen that animals use and taking up the carbon dioxide they release. There is even an energy cycle where plants make energy from the sun and provide food for animals, which then release their nitrogen back into the environment when they die. That nitrogen is used to nourish new growing plants all over again. These cycles are how our environment is balanced.

Though the environment is in balance in many ways, it does change over time. Glaciers advance and retreat. Temperatures change, animals go extinct, and animals evolve. The continents slowly drift over millions of years. Volcanoes erupt and spew carbon dioxide into the air. Hurricanes flatten forests and change the shape of shorelines.

Though our planet may seem like a vast and powerful place, we are changing the earth's environment all the time too. There are over 6 billion people on Earth and our activities do affect the environment. We dam rivers, clear-cut forests, drain lakes, and create deserts. Interestingly, we may affect the planet in ways that actually will come back and hurt us!

This book will tell you about the environment, how it varies in different habitats, and how you affect it. You can see how people are trying to protect the environment and how you can make a difference. If you want to know how to protect the environment and get involved in being more "green," that is called environmentalism. It's cool to be an environmentalist and our environment needs you!

# TryThis

## A Worm's Environment— A Cup of Dirt

**Make a model of an earthworm's environment, and a great party dessert too!**

1.  Pour 2 cups of cold milk into a large bowl.
2.  Add 1 package of chocolate-flavored instant pudding and pie filling.
3.  Beat with a whisk until well mixed.
4.  Stir in one 8-ounce tub of whipped topping.
5.  Then stir in ½ cup crushed chocolate sandwich cookies.
6.  Divide mixture into ten clear, plastic cups.
7.  Sprinkle more crushed chocolate sandwich cookies on top.
8.  Keep cold in the fridge.
9.  Right before serving push a gummy worm into each cup.

## Describe Your Environment

Sit in a circle and take turns naming an animal or plant. Then the person to your right has to name 5–10 traits of the environment of that suggested animal or plant. For example, if they say, "cactus," you might say, "sand, heat, lizard, tortoise, rocks, rattlesnake, wind, scorpion, vulture, roadrunner."

# What Is the Environment?

The answer may surprise you. The environment is all living and nonliving things on Earth. Your indoor environment includes your family, pets, and houseplants, but it also includes the furniture, floors, windows, and even the air temperature around you. If you go outside your environment changes to the trees, grass, insects, birds, clouds, wind, and ground. Environments can be big or small. If you are a beetle, your environment could just be a rotten log or a vegetable garden. If you are a lake trout your environment is the sand, rocks, lily pads, ducks, water striders, and the very water you live in. That is just one reason why it is important to keep lakes and streams clean and free from dumping. The things humans add to a water environment affect everything in it. And it's the only environment they've got!

## Our Little Blue Ball–The Birth of Environmentalism

When astronauts brought back the first color pictures of Earth from space, it had an intense effect on humankind. It was the first time people could see the planet as the beautiful and fragile place it was. That picture stirred people to help preserve the earth and its amazing beauty in a way that nothing else ever had. Since that time, there has been an ongoing struggle to preserve our planet's natural beauty and clean resources while still having enough food, energy, and land for our more than 6 billion people to live.

## Your Green Footprints

Being aware of how your actions affect the planet is the first step in conservation and being "green." How much land and water it takes for each of us to survive is called our "ecological footprint." How big a footprint you leave depends upon how much of the planet's resources you use up. There are many ways you can help conserve

# Here It Comes Again

An important message has been put into a puzzle grid and cut into six pieces. Can you figure out where each piece goes and write the letters into the empty grid?

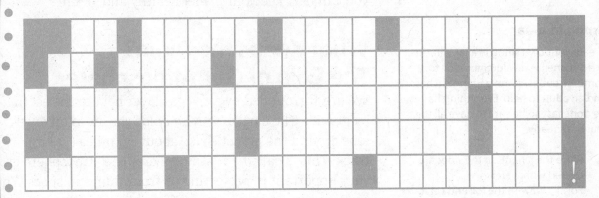

## Environmental Experiment

### Smog in a Jar

Create your own smog in a jar. All you need is one jar, an aluminum foil top, some ice cubes, some paper, matches, and an adult to help. Everything has to be done fast so be sure to have all the materials ready.

1. Rinse the jar out, so the sides are coated with water.
2. Form a lid with the foil and set it aside with the ice cubes on top to cool.
3. Have your adult helper light the paper and drop it into the jar. Quickly put on the cold foil lid with the ice cubes on top.
4. See how the smoke sits on the bottom of the jar? This is the way smog forms.
5. Don't breathe it in when you release your smog outside. It's bad for you!

resources and keep our planet clean and healthy for generations to come. This is called "thinking green." To be an environmentalist and "live green," you first have to understand how the environment works. Read on to learn about our planet's atmosphere, habitats, and resources, and how we affect them. By the end of this book you will know how you can help keep our planet healthy and green!

## What Keeps the Air In? The Role of Our Atmosphere

We are surrounded by air, a gas layer held to the earth by gravity. The earth's gravity holds the air in an envelope around the planet that's about 6.5 miles (11 km) thick. This is called our atmosphere. The atmosphere is very important in protecting us from things in space. The moon is covered with craters from being bombarded by meteors because it has no atmosphere to protect it. Most meteors that might have hit the earth burn up in the atmosphere before reaching us. All we see is the streak of light as meteors burn up as shooting stars.

The atmosphere also protects us from the fierce ultraviolet light from the sun. It absorbs much of this light and lets just enough through to warm and nourish us. The atmosphere keeps us from getting too hot when our side of the planet faces the sun on a summer day or too cold when we are facing away from the sun on a winter night. It may sound like the atmosphere knows just what we need, but in truth, life on Earth evolved the way it did because our atmosphere provided the exact conditions we needed to live.

### The Atmospheric Layer Cake

The earth's atmosphere is divided into five layers. The layers closest to the earth are the thickest and then get thinner and fade into space. A rocket leaving our atmosphere would have to go through each layer to get to space. When a rocket launches from Earth it starts in the first layer, the troposphere. It is in this level of the atmosphere where all our weather occurs. This is where clouds form, as well as lightning, high winds, hurricanes, tornadoes, snow, hail, and freezing rain. It's a busy, bumpy place!

Next a rocket would pass through the stratosphere where the air is calmer. This is where airplanes travel because the air is much less bouncy at this altitude. It is also where ultraviolet radiation from the sun reacts with oxygen to form ozone gas and the ozone layer. The ozone layer protects us from getting too much harmful radiation from the sun.

Next the rocket would fly through the mesosphere, the layer of the atmosphere that stops most meteors as they fly toward Earth. Then the rocket would reach the thermosphere. This is where the space shuttle orbits the earth. Then it would go through the exosphere, which is the outermost boundary of our atmosphere. This is where satellites orbit. From here a rocket would leave Earth's atmosphere and begin its journey into space.

## WORDS to KNOW

**OZONE-DEPLETING GASES:**
Ozone-depleting gases are CFCs found in refrigerants, aerosols, solvents, methyl bromide fumigant, and halon.

**SMOG:** Smog is ground level ozone and particulate matter formed by burning fuels on hot, sunny days. The word *smog* came from the combination of the words *smoke* and *fog*.

## The Ozone Layer

Ozone in the atmosphere protects the earth from the sun's powerful ultraviolet radiation. This blanket of

## What Can Be Done

### Help Save the Ozone Layer

Everyone can pitch in to help stop ozone destruction in our atmosphere. Here are some simple tips. For more tips visit the EPA Web site at: *www.epa.gov/ozone*.

1. Ask your parents to make sure your air conditioners are in good condition and aren't leaking coolant. When they buy a new air conditioner, ask them to buy one that uses non-ozone-depleting refrigerant. Tell them no R-22 refrigerant!

2. Ask your parents to make sure when their car air conditioner gets serviced that the refrigerants are recovered and recycled, and not released into the air.

3. Ask your parents to make sure that before they throw away old refrigerators, air conditioners, and dehumidifiers, they have the refrigerants recovered and recycled and not released into the air. (They can ask the local trash collector if the refrigerant will be recovered and recycled before the appliance is thrown away.)

protection is called the ozone layer. Over the last twenty-five years something has been breaking down the protective ozone layer. Scientists discovered that chemical compounds called CFCs (chlorofluorocarbons), that are in aerosol sprays and refrigerants, were actually destroying the ozone faster than it could be replaced. In 1978, the United States banned the use of products that released CFCs into the atmosphere. According to the EPA, collecting the refrigerant out of old refrigerators alone, before throwing them out, would prevent about 4 million pounds of CFCs from being sent into the atmosphere each year.

### There's a Hole in Our Ozone!

When an actual "ozone hole" was discovered over the Antarctic in the early 1980s, scientists knew stronger steps would have to be taken worldwide to protect the ozone layer. In 1987 an international agreement called the Montreal Protocol was made between 180 nations on Earth to stop making and using the ozone-depleting gases. If these countries keep their promise, the ozone layer will recover over time. Some scientists estimate that it will take about fifty years.

### Bad Ozone

Not all ozone is good. When ozone forms on the ground, it is harmful to people, crops, and trees. Ozone forms on the ground when exhaust from cars, factories, and chemicals mix with strong sunlight and hot temperatures. This bad combination creates harmful smog. Smog can cause serious breathing problems. Some cities have ozone alerts where they

# Water Warning

If rain falls on an environment that has been contaminated (made dirty with chemicals) it won't be safe to drink. You can help prevent this! Figure out which two extra words appear over and over in the puzzle grid. Cross out all the extra words and read the remaining message!

CLEAN NEVER DRINK POUR CLEAN CHEMICALS DRINK
LIKE CLEAN PAINT, DRINK PESTICIDES, CLEAN OR
DRINK OIL CLEAN ON DRINK THE CLEAN GROUND.
DRINK RAIN CLEAN CAN DRINK WASH CLEAN THEM
DRINK DOWN CLEAN THE DRINK STORM CLEAN DRAIN
DRINK OR CLEAN THROUGH DRINK THE CLEAN SOIL
CLEAN INTO DRINK THE CLEAN WATER DRINK SUPPLY!

The EVERYTHING KIDS' Environment Book

suggest that people stay indoors and not exercise when smog levels are high.

# Do You Get My Drift? How the Earth's Continents Formed

Millions of years ago our continents were not shaped the way they are today. As a matter of fact, they were not separate continents at all! Scientists now believe that the earth's land masses were once all one giant land mass called Pangaea. Over the last 250 million years the continents have broken up and drifted to where they are today. Scientists call this Continental Drift.

If you look at all the continents on a map, you can see how they all once fit together. Try it! Copy a map and cut out all the continents. Now try and piece them together looking at a map of Pangaea as a guide. Can you make the first supercontinent?

## Is the Ground Moving Under Us?

The continents drift because the ground under your feet is not made up of the solid, unmoving land you might think. The earth's crust is made up of a series of plates. Over time the plates move, though very slowly—sometimes less than an inch a year. This is called "plate tectonics." It may not seem like much, but the movement of these plates is what forms mountain ranges and volcanoes, and causes earthquakes. When the edges of two plates collide, they can form a mountain range. Don't get out your hiking books yet—this takes millions of years. When two underwater plates move away from each other, that forms a mid-ocean ridge. Sometimes two plates slide over one another. This forms a fault, like the San Andreas Fault in California.

## Whose "Fault" Is That Volcano?

Plate movement at a fault can cause earthquakes and volcanic activity like the eruption of Mount St. Helens

# TryThis

### Create Your Own Volcanic Eruption

**You will need one old mayonnaise jar, some baking soda, liquid dish soap, ketchup (optional), vinegar, and a sandy pile in your yard (optional). The carbon dioxide that is released when you mix the baking soda and vinegar is like a volcanic gas eruption!**

1. Put the jar in the sink, or in a lasagna pan that can collect the "lava flow." You can bury the jar in a volcano-shaped pile of sand in your yard if you want to make this look like a real volcanic eruption. Maybe try it in the sink first as a trial run.
2. Add ⅛ cup baking soda to the jar.
3. Squirt in some liquid soap.
4. Pour in ⅛ cup vinegar (you can mix the ketchup in with the vinegar before you add it, if you want to make the lava flow look red).
5. Stand back and watch your volcanic eruption!

# TryThis

## WORDS to KNOW

**AQUIFER:** Aquifers are places underground where water flows through sand, gravel, or even clay. People drill wells hoping to hit an aquifer for a good flow of water.

in Washington State in 1980. There are more than 500 active volcanoes in the world and most of them are found where two plates come together. Volcanic eruptions are most dangerous because of the toxic gases they release. Volcanic eruptions are thought to be responsible for putting about 110 million tons of carbon dioxide into the atmosphere every year—all resulting from some drifting plates!

# Water, Water Everywhere— The Water Cycle

The water cycle is how we keep our precious water supply on Earth. It has no beginning and no end. It goes around and around and around and has for billions of years. In truth, the amount of water on Earth has stayed pretty much the same, but its location and form does change over time. To explore the water cycle, we'll start with one section, but it is not the beginning, it is just part of the ongoing cycle.

## The Many Faces of Water

Water exists in three forms: liquid, solid (ice), and gas. All three forms of water can be seen in everyday life. Drinking a glass of ice water on a hot day can show you all three. The water in your glass is the liquid, the ice is the solid, and the wetness on the outside of your glass is the water vapor cooling back to liquid right before your very eyes! This is called "condensation." In any of those forms, water is still water. It can take part in the water cycle. Water can be found in the ocean, polar ice caps, as rivers, lakes, wetlands, and snow on land, as underground aquifers, and even in the air as water vapor in the clouds. The sun drives the water cycle by evaporating water into its rising vapor form. Then it cycles back as rain or snow to start again!

## Making Clouds

Clouds form when water vapor, heated by the sun, rises off the earth by evaporation. The water vapor condenses in the cooler air that is higher up in the atmosphere. It clings to small particles in the air like dust or pollen. When the water condenses into clouds it is changing back from vapor to liquid. You can see condensation all around you on the earth. Just look at dew-covered grass or your fogged-up ski goggles. Condensation happens when warm water vapor meets cooler air and turns back to a liquid.

When you drive through a patch of fog, you are actually driving through a cloud that has formed right on the surface of the earth. This happens when very moist, warm air meets cool air and the water condenses right on the spot as fog!

## Making Rain

The clouds gather all the tiny water droplets and crash them together until they are big enough to fall as rain or snow. This is precipitation. Precipitation varies throughout the planet. It rains much more in warm, tropical places than in deserts. In colder places precipitation falls as snow instead of rain. When rain falls on land, it soaks into the ground and adds to the groundwater. This is the fresh drinking water for people throughout the world. Rain also runs into rivers and streams, which make their way to the ocean, our largest body of water.

## Storing Water on Earth

The oceans store 95 percent of our planet's water. Oceans, rivers, and lakes together make up about 90 percent of all the water that evaporates into the atmosphere. The other 10 percent comes from plants losing water (transpiration), and a tiny amount from glacial ice evaporating (sublimation). With the process of evaporation, we have come back to where we started in the water cycle.

**WORDS to KNOW**

**PRECIPITATION:** Precipitation is when water falls from the sky in the form of rain, snow, hail, sleet, or freezing rain.

**GROUNDWATER:** Groundwater is the water that flows underground filling soil and flowing out into springs and aquifers.

## Environmental Experiment

### Plants and the Water Cycle

You will need a plastic bag, a twist tie, and a tree or bush in your yard.

1. Take a gallon-sized plastic bag and cover a small branch—leaves and all—with it.
2. Close it tightly with the twist tie.
3. Come back the next day and look at it. There should be water in the bag with the twig. This is the water the plant lost in transpiration. Normally it would have evaporated into the water cycle.

### Create Your Own Water Cycle

**If you have ever looked at a terrarium, you have seen a tiny water cycle in action. You can create this effect easily yourself.**

1. Take a small, empty jar with a lid. Line the bottom with small pebbles and then about an inch of soil.
2. Then go out in the woods and dig up a small patch of plants. It can be any plants—weeds are fine. Include a little moss or not, just make sure you have a bunch of green plant life.
3. Water your plant until you can see the water covering the pebbles at the bottom.
4. Then put on the lid and set it in the sun.
5. Watch your terrarium. Within a day or two, the water will condense on the sides of the jar. From this point forward you will not have to water your terrarium. It has its own water cycle!

## How Glaciers Form

In some places, like Antarctica and Greenland, more snow falls than melts. Over time the deep snow presses into ice. Water can be stored in glaciers for a long time until the earth's climate warms. Then the ice will melt and be released into the water cycle again. During the last ice age, glaciers covered much of North America, northern Europe, and Asia. Even now 10 percent of Earth's land is covered by glacial ice. Glacial ice is fresh water compared to the salt water of our oceans. Glaciers store more than half of all the fresh water on Earth. As global warming affects our planet we are seeing even Greenland and Antarctica's ice packs melting.

## Global Warming

*Global warming* is a term used to describe an increase in Earth's temperature from, in part, humans releasing large amounts of carbon dioxide into the air. Scientists believe that this will lead to climate change (a warmer Earth) that will have many bad effects on living things on the planet, including us! Some changes scientists think may occur include changes in rainfall patterns, melting glaciers, rising sea levels, and numerous other impacts on animals and plants. More on this topic can be found in Chapter 4.

# Take a Deep Breath— The Oxygen Cycle

Living things need oxygen to survive. We inhale oxygen and exhale carbon dioxide. This is called respiration. Plants then take that carbon dioxide, convert it into carbohydrates, and release oxygen. Then we use that oxygen, and the cycle continues. Animals, plants, and even bacteria also use oxygen. When plants and animals die and decompose, that process uses oxygen too. Oxygen is used when you burn a fire. Even rusting metal uses oxygen. (This is called oxidation.) Oxygen is needed for processes all over the planet! With so many living things breathing all the oxygen on Earth, you would think we might run out, but luckily more oxygen is being made all the time in the oxygen cycle.

### How Plants Help Us Breathe

The oxygen cycle never stops, but where does oxygen come from? Mostly oxygen comes from photosynthesis. Both plants on land and phytoplankton (tiny, microscopic plants floating on the surface of the ocean) use photosynthesis to make energy. They also make oxygen! Photosynthesis is a process where the organism uses sunlight, carbon dioxide, and water to make oxygen and sugar. Thank goodness for green plants and other photosynthesizers!

## Hungry Anyone?
## The Energy Cycle

Every living thing on Earth needs energy to live. Not all organisms get it the same way. Only plants can make their own energy with photosynthesis. Animals must eat plants or other animals to survive. When animals and plants die, their bodies decompose and release their nutrients back to the environment. The nutrients they release when they decompose can be used to nourish new plants. They also nourish decomposers. Decomposers include insects, bacteria, fungi, and other microorganisms. All these animals and plants are part of the energy cycle.

If you look at a simple food web, it tells the story of how interconnected we are on Earth. Plants, because they make their own energy,

## Great Idea!

There is a very simple way to save a lot of energy in your home. If you do, that means there is a lot more energy that can be used somewhere else! Break the Last-to-First Code to learn more.

ompactC luorescentf

ightl ulbsb seu ne-o

uarterq

fo het

lectricitye

hatt a

egularr

ightl

ulbb

sesu.

# TryThis

**Predator-Prey Tag**

Learn about food webs while playing a game of tag. Get together with a few friends and each choose an animal to be. You can be a plant, a herbivore, a carnivore, or an omnivore. The herbivores can chase the plants. The carnivores can chase the herbivores. The omnivores can chase the plants and herbivores. Run around and have fun hunting!

are called producers. Plants are eaten by herbivores, like rabbits, mice, and deer. Carnivores, from weasels to mountain lions, eat other animals, usually the herbivores. Some animals eat both plants and animals. They are called omnivores. Many carnivores, like bears, actually eat both plants and animals, and so have an omnivorous diet. When plants or animals die, decomposers eat them. All living things form a complex web of interconnected diets. The food web!

# Chapter 2
# Habitats of the World

# The Rainforest

There are rainforests all around the world. Though a rainforest in South America may have many different types of animals and plants from a rainforest in Africa, what they all do have in common is: heat, humidity, rain, and very tall trees. Rainforests get at least 80 inches (200 cm) of rain per year and have an average temperature of about 80°F (26°C). Rainforest trees are so tall because they are competing for the sunlight they need in a forest thick with vegetation.

All this heat, moisture, and humidity make a very fertile environment. Scientists believe that rainforests may contain more than half of all the earth's species of animals and plants. This is called biodiversity. The rainforest is famous for its biodiversity because it has so many different species, and a lot of them haven't even been discovered yet!

## Did You Know?

### Your Plants Are from the Rainforest!

Many houseplants found in American homes actually came from the rainforest originally, like philodendrons, orchids, and bromeliads. Rainforest plants are adapted to survive in the dim sunlight under the thick forest canopy. That's a perfect trait for a plant that will live in your living room and only get a little light.

## Rainforests Help You Breathe!

Rainforests are very valuable to our global environment because their dense greenery collects more sunlight than any other habitat in the world. There is a lot of photosynthesis going on in the rainforest and that is a big part of the oxygen cycle. Think of all those trees taking in carbon dioxide and releasing the oxygen we need. Rainforests are like giant, green filters for our atmosphere.

## Losing Our Rainforests

Rainforests are also valuable because of their many kinds of animals, plants, and giant trees. Rainforests all over the world are being cut for timber. When the trees are gone, all the animals, insects, and plants go too. The environment is totally changed. The humidity that clung to the trees evaporates away. Erosion washes the thin soil away. Rainforest land is often cleared and burned for farmland, even though the soil is thin and not very

good for growing crops. It is estimated that more than 35 million acres of rainforest are being cleared every year. Since rainforests are so important for decreasing carbon dioxide and creating oxygen for the oxygen cycle, no one knows for sure what will happen when all the rainforests are gone.

Many of the animals on the endangered species list live in rainforests. They include:

- Aye-aye
- Chimpanzee
- Gibbon
- Gorilla
- Jaguar
- Lemur
- Ocelot
- Orangutan
- Mountain tapir
- Tiger

### Ecotourism

Many countries, like Costa Rica, have discovered how saving their rainforests can make them money! The beautiful rainforest habitat brings tourists into Costa Rica to see wild places. This is called ecotourism and is a great way to get countries to save some of their vanishing forests. Costa Rica has put aside 12 percent of its land as wild rainforest. It may not seem like much, but that area of rainforest will be protected and that is a very good thing.

## The Deserts

The word *desert* often brings to mind endless miles of scorching sand dunes, but in truth deserts vary in both landscape and temperature. The Sahara desert, the largest hot desert in the world, is a sizzling belt of sand dunes that stretches the whole width of Africa. It can reach more than 125°F (51°C) during the day, with powerful winds. At night, with no plant life to hold the heat,

**WORDS to KNOW**

**ECOTOURISM:** Ecotourism is when people visit a place to see the exotic wildlife and natural habitats. Many countries use ecotourism money to help their economy while protecting their natural habitats.

# Environmental Experiment

### Make Your Own Rain Shower

Rainforests are hot and steamy. Steamy air rises and hits the cooler air above, causing rain. You can make your own tropical rain shower. You need two pie pans, ice cubes, an oven mitt, cold water, an electric (plug in) teapot, and help from a grownup.

1. Plug in the kettle full of water. Place an empty pie pan on the countertop in front of its spout.
2. Add cold water and ice cubes to the other pie pan.
3. When the teapot boils put on your oven mitt to protect your hand and hold the pie pan full of ice water up over the steam rising out of the teapot spout.
4. The water vapor will begin to collect on the bottom of the ice-chilled pie pan. It will cool and condense. Soon water droplets will begin to drip down into the bottom pie pan.
5. You have just created a rain shower!

# Paper Trail

Less than half of the paper products we use are recovered for recycling. We can do better than that! See if you can find all the paper products hiding in the grid. Highlight each one with a bright marker. Next time you go to throw this item out at your house, save it for recycling instead! Words can be up and down, side to side, or backwards.

CEREAL BOX
ENVELOPE
JUNK MAIL
SHIPPING CARTON
WRAPPING PAPER
LUNCH BAG
EGG CARTON
DECORATIONS
COMPUTER PRINTOUTS
OLD BOOKS
MAGAZINES
POSTER
PIZZA BOX
CATALOGS
GREETING CARDS
PHONE BOOK
NEWSPAPER

```
K I A G A B H C N U L O X
X Z O L D B O O K S B M C
O Z X J U N K M A I L A K
B U N K R O X P Z A S G S
A D E S E P I U N Z H A D
Z N N N P O S T E R I Z R
Z O V O A F K E W G P I A
I T E I P X I R S K P N C
P R L T G H A P P O I E G
J A O A N Z Z R A O N S N
K C P R I L Z I P B G X I
M G E O P O X N E E C I T
U G N C P K N T R N A Z E
C E R E A L B O X O R Z E
O P Q D R R S U T H T P R
Z Z I P W A U T V P O U G
C A T A L O G S O X N N X
```

the Sahara can drop to below freezing. Not all of the Sahara desert is made up of sandy dunes. Its landscape can vary from gravelly flats to mountains, and dotted here and there are precious oases, which hold the only water and most plant life found in the Sahara. Oases have allowed some people and animals to make a small living in the desert.

To live in a desert, plants and animals have to adapt to survive. Many animals are nocturnal and only become active at night when the air is cooler. Some animals go into a type of hibernation and sleep through times of drought or extreme heat. This is called estivation. Some animals like the fennec fox develop large ears to cool off their bodies. The way this works is that the blood circulating through the ears is very close to the surface and is cooled by chilly nighttime desert temperatures. Some other desert animals can survive without drinking any water at all, but get all the moisture they need from the dry plants they eat.

Many of the animals on the endangered species list live in the desert. Some include:

- Arabian oryx
- Bactrian camel
- Desert bandicoot
- Desert monitor
- Desert tortoise
- Fresno kangaroo rat
- San Esteban Island chuckwalla
- Sonoran pronghorn

## Deserts: Lands of Extremes

The hot, central Australian desert has red sand plains, mountains, and bluffs spotted with dry lake beds that shimmer in the sun with the false promise of water showing in superheated mirages. Amazingly, many animals like kangaroos have adapted to the dry landscape and can survive from the little moisture they get in the plants they eat.

# TryThis

## Make Their Environment

Find pictures of animals in old magazines and trace them (or cut them out and paste them) onto the center of a large sheet of paper. Now draw their environment around them. For example, if you have traced an African elephant, add the grassy savannah. Add a baobab tree and a bright blue sky. Add a herd of zebras and a giraffe. This is an elephant environment.

The Sonoran Desert has large, sandy plains and bleak mountains. It stretches over parts of southern California, Arizona, and northwestern Mexico. Branches of the Colorado River run through it, so many trees, cacti, and shrubs find enough water to grow there. In Arizona, the giant saguaro and barrel cactuses can be seen all over the desert. Beautiful flowering cacti and yucca make the desert seem more like a garden than the open sandy place one might imagine. When deserts do get rain, plants bloom and seed quickly to take advantage of the short-lived water supply. Heavy rains can cause flash floods and a dry riverbed can be a gushing river in just a few minutes. The desert is a habitat of extremes!

### Cold Deserts

The largest desert on Earth is actually not a hot desert at all but a freezing ice shelf—the interior of Antarctica. Though covered with ice, it rarely snows here. Most of the snow falls on the coasts. This frozen desert, oddly enough, keeps much of the earth's fresh water locked in a thick sheet of ice more than a mile thick. Another cold desert is the barren, rocky plain between southern Mongolia and northern China called the Gobi desert.

The world's deserts are growing. A dry grassland is just a few inches of rain away from becoming a desert. When overgrazed by livestock, the plants, whose roots have stabilized the soil and held in the moisture, are lost. The topsoil dries up and is blown or washed away. The land becomes a desert.

## The Grasslands

Grasslands (also called prairies) are found between forests and deserts throughout the world. They are wetter habitats than deserts but much drier than rainforests. There might be a few trees here and there on a grassland, but mostly it is just grass. Since there are not many trees to use for nesting or escaping predators, a lot of grassland animals can run very fast. On the African

# Recycled Words

We think of recycling as a new idea, but over 2000 years ago, the Chinese recycled old fishing nets and rags to make paper! The list below is full of items that can be recycled. See if you can use all the letters to spell new words, using the clues provided.

GLASS    **STEEL**    PLASTIC

**PAPER**    ALUMINUM    **VEGGIE SCRAPS**

1. They hold teeth in your mouth = _ _ _ _

2. They are delicious hard-boiled = _ _ _ _

3. A thin piece of cheese or meat = _ _ _ _ _

4. Squares of hard, colored clay = _ _ _ _ _

5. Where you go to sleep in a tent = _ _ _ _

6. Liquid from a tree used to make syrup = _ _ _

7. Fruit with small top and round bottom = _ _ _ _

8. Conceited about your looks = _ _ _ _

9. Look at long and hard = _ _ _ _ _

10. Opposite of "push" = _ _ _ _

grassland, called the savannah, herds of zebra, gazelle, and ostrich graze together, all sharing the responsibility of watching for predators. Wildebeest herds can reach more than a million members. It's safer to live in a group! The predators are fast too. The African cheetah, thought to be the fastest mammal on Earth, can reach speeds of 70 mph (112 km) in short spurts.

## Life on the Australian Grasslands

On the dry, scrubby, Australian grasslands, animals are very fast too, but they get away by hopping! Kangaroos travel in groups, called mobs, at up to 35 mph (56 km). The dry Australian grassland, often called the outback, is home to many species of wildlife besides the kangaroo. Here travelers can find dingoes, bandicoots, fringed lizards, and wallabies.

## Grassland or Farmland?

Grasslands are some of the most fertile lands on Earth. Much of our planet's grasslands have been plowed as farmland, because the soil is so good for growing food. That is why these areas have been named the breadbasket of the world. These lands are also good for cattle and horses to feed in great herds. So much grassland has been plowed over, that people began to worry these lands would disappear completely. Some short and tall grass prairies are now protected from development in small prairie preserves, and Africa has made national parks to try and protect disappearing wildlife that were being replaced by domestic livestock. In the future, we will have to make a balance between keeping some natural grasslands for the wildlife and using others for growing the food we need.

Many of the animals on the endangered species list live on the grasslands, including:

- African elephant
- African wild ass
- African wild dog

The EVERYTHING KIDS' Environment Book

- Arabian gazelle
- Black-footed ferret
- Cheetah
- Giant sable antelope
- Przewalski's horse
- Tibetan antelope
- Woodland caribou

### Prairies and Fire

Prairie fires are an important way for grasslands to renew themselves. Some plants need fire to make their seeds sprout. The burned grass acts as a fertilizer for the next plants coming up. Large animals can outrun the flames, but smaller animals escape fire (and predators) by seeking safety in burrows underground. Here they are safe from raging prairie fires that sweep across the plains. The

American prairie dog lives in large colonies and never strays far from the opening of its safe burrow. Only animals that can enter their tunnels, like rattlesnakes and black-footed ferrets, can get at a prairie dog inside its home.

## Wetlands

Wetlands are one of the most varied habitats, home to many kinds of animals and plants. They are very important for wildlife because there is a lot of food in a wetland. Many species of birds breed and raise their young in wetlands. Ducks, geese, swans, and loons are among the birds that migrate between wetlands in the north and south all year. The abundance of water makes wetlands ideal habitats for insects and the animals that eat them, like bats

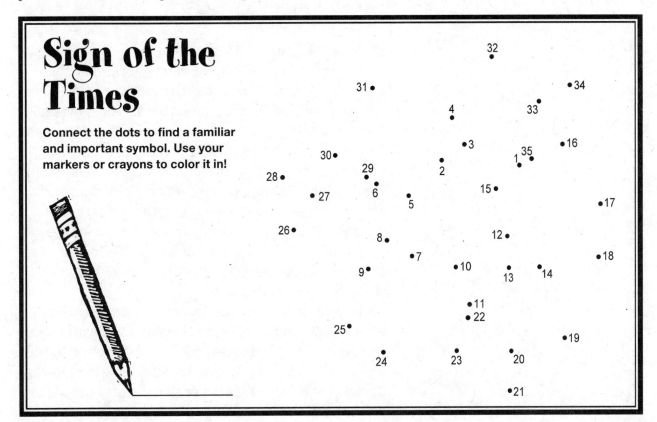

# Sign of the Times

**Connect the dots to find a familiar and important symbol. Use your markers or crayons to color it in!**

**Did You Know?**

**Bog Mummies**

Some bogs are so acidic that when a human body is found in one they are often preserved almost like a mummy, even if they are hundreds of years old. The oldest body found in a bog was in Denmark and is thought to be 10,000 years old!

and swallows, and amphibians like frogs and salamanders. Reptiles, such as turtles, snakes, and alligators, are also common in wetlands. With so many animals breeding in wetlands, mammal predators often roam there looking for prey. They are habitats rich with wildlife.

Many of the animals on the endangered species list live in wetlands, including:

- Alaotra grebe
- Aquatic box turtle
- Atlantic, Chinook, Coho, sockeye, and chum salmon
- Bog turtle
- California tiger salamander
- Catfish
- Hawaiian common moorhen
- Spotted pond turtle
- Steelhead trout
- Sturgeon

## Many Kinds of Wetlands

Though all wetlands have water in common, there are many different kinds of wetlands in the world. There are marshes that are often found on the edges of ponds and lakes. Marshes are open wetlands dotted with reeds, sedges, and grass, like cattails. Swamps, on the other hand, are often thick with shrubs and even trees. Walking through a swamp can be hard and even dangerous. Mangrove swamps form along coastlines where rivers meet the sea. The water there is brackish, which means that it is a little salty, but not as salty as the ocean. Mangroves are important for protecting shorelines from storm flooding and erosion.

Bogs form from shallow ponds that have slowly collected plants and leaves until they are thick with them and other plants like moss and ferns root right over the water in the rotting plant matter. Over time this makes a thick mat on top of the water that is called peat. Like plastic wrap over a bowl, no air can get in and the rotting plants beneath build up acids. As a result things that fall into bogs rot very, very slowly. These are just a few of the many kinds of wetlands in the world.

### Watch Out for Hungry Plants

Wetlands have so much water that the soil can actually be washed free of its nutrients. Plants have to be adapted to a water habitat to survive there. A few kinds of plants have adapted and get extra nutrients by trapping and absorbing insects! Pitcher plants, sundews, and Venus flytraps all are insectivorous plants found in wetlands. Each plant has its own amazing adaptation for trapping insect prey.

Pitcher plants trap insects by having a sweet smell and red lines running down inside the pitcherlike leaves like a runway. Insects follow the lines down into the pitcher looking for nectar. When they try to get out, they find stiff hairs pointing down, blocking their escape. Soon they get tired and fall into the acidic liquid in the bottom of the pitcher where they dissolve over time.

Sundews have sticky fluid on their hairy leaves that insects mistake for nectar. When an insect lands on the leaf it gets stuck in the goo and then the leaf rolls up with the insect inside and dissolves it.

Venus flytraps have a really cool adaptation for catching insects. At the end of each leaf stalk is a clamshell-shaped leaf that lies open with a red-colored inside to attract insects. An insect landing inside the leaf will trip a hair trigger that snaps the leaf closed. The insect, now trapped inside, gets dissolved by the plant.

## The Oceans

If you look at a map of the world you can see many different oceans, but in fact they are all connected, covering three-fourths of the earth. The Pacific is the largest ocean, followed by the Atlantic, Indian, Southern, and Arctic Oceans. Oceans are so vast and huge that they have many different kinds of habitats in them. The surface of the

**WORDS to KNOW**

**INSECTIVOROUS:** Insectivorous plants are plants that trap and digest insects as added food.

ocean, where sunlight can reach, is called the epipelagic zone. It is where most sea life is found. Here millions upon millions of tiny phytoplankton float along, making their living on the energy of the sun using photosynthesis. They are at the bottom of the food chain in the ocean and many animals feed on them. In this layer of the ocean we find most of the fish, sharks, rays, jellyfish, marine mammals, and sea turtles.

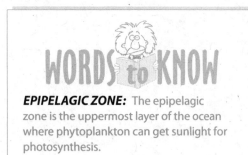

**WORDS to KNOW**

**EPIPELAGIC ZONE:** The epipelagic zone is the uppermost layer of the ocean where phytoplankton can get sunlight for photosynthesis.

An ocean habitat that is rarely seen by humans is the bottom of the ocean, or the benthic zone. Animals here have to be able to live in total darkness and survive the fierce water pressure. Some have adapted with some strange survival traits, like glowing in the dark!

## The Rich Reef

Another ocean habitat is the coral reef. After rainforests, coral reefs are thought to have the most biodiversity of any kind of habitat. That means they have a huge number of animals and plants living there. They are a rich and important habitat.

Many of the animals on the endangered species list live in the oceans, including:

- Blue whale
- Bowhead whale
- Finback whale
- Gray whale
- Green sea turtle
- Hawaiian monk seal
- Hawksbill sea turtle
- Humpback whale
- Leatherback sea turtle
- Loggerhead sea turtle
- Sperm whale
- Steller's sea lion

### Tidy Ocean Habitat

Tide pools are another distinct ocean habitat. They are found where the oceans meet the shorelines. The low tide zone has the most species, as it gets sun, water, and is for the most part beyond the pounding waves. Animals in tidal zones have to adapt to wave action by developing anchors so they won't get washed away, plus be able to move to stay wet in the changing tide. That's a lot of adapting!

## The Polar Regions

Antarctica is the coldest place on Earth, sometimes reaching 130 degrees below 0°F. It is one of our seven continents and includes the South Pole. The coast of Antarctica is windy and snow-covered, yet inland the Antarctic is a desert! The dry Antarctic interior is not like a hot sand desert at all, though it is considered the driest place on Earth. It is actually covered by a sheet of ice a mile or more thick, but there is rarely snowfall. It is a frozen desert. The Antarctic ice sheets may hold about 90 percent of all the earth's fresh water! Penguins, fur seals, leopard seals, Weddell seals, elephant seals, albatross, petrels, blue whales, killer whales, and krill all make their homes on or in the southern ocean around the frozen continent.

## WORDS to KNOW

**PERMAFROST:** Permafrost is the layer of soil just below the surface that stays frozen year round, mostly in the polar regions of the earth.

## TryThis

**Polar Bear Freeze**

Fill up an ice cube tray with blue raspberry juice (light blue colored). Then add three gummy bears to each ice cube spot. Let them freeze for several hours. Invite friends over and pop a couple of ice cubes into a little glass bowl for each person with a spoon. Polar bear freeze treats for all!

The Arctic doesn't contain a central land mass like the Antarctic, but includes the northern edges of Europe, Asia, North America, and Greenland, and, of course, also contains the North Pole. So it's mostly frozen ocean—nine feet thick frozen ocean! The only land habitat in the Arctic is called arctic tundra, treeless, frozen land covered in permafrost that only grows plants in the twenty-four-hour sun of the short Arctic summer. This boggy plain is not an easy place to travel, especially when the fierce mosquitoes descend to feed on the animals living there. Musk ox, caribou, lemming, arctic fox, hare, wolf, and polar bear all fall prey to the biting insects of the Arctic.

## Understanding Icebergs

Icebergs are huge chunks of ice that float in the ocean. They form in the warmer months when they calve off a glacier or ice pack. Most icebergs come from the edges of the Antarctic or Greenland ice sheets, so are made of fresh water. They are usually a lot bigger than they look. The saying that something is "the tip of

## TryThis

### Hidden Danger

You can easily show the hidden nature of icebergs. Take a clear glass bowl and fill it with water. Drop in an ice cube. Notice how much of the ice cube shows above the water—not very much. Now imagine that ice cube is the size of your entire school building!

the iceberg" means that you are just seeing a little bit above the water. Usually only about one-eighth of the iceberg is showing above the water. Most of it is hidden underwater out of sight. This can be a hazard to passing ships. Interestingly, it is the smaller icebergs, called growlers, that can be the most dangerous because they don't show up on a ship's radar and can't be seen easily from above water.

## Urban Environments

Though you don't often think of cities as having wild areas, in fact green spaces in urban areas can have a multitude of animal and plant life. Even a patch of weeds in an abandoned lot can have insects like butterflies, moths, ants, bees, beetles, and even cockroaches. Wild mammals like mice, rats, raccoons, skunks, squirrels, chipmunks, bats, and even deer are not unusual in urban settings. Songbirds, pigeons, hawks, peregrine falcons, ducks, and seagulls can also be common. Even reptiles and amphibians can be found in and near city park ponds.

Wildlife in urban areas have adapted to city life as if it were a wild habitat. Pigeons that once nested on cliffs and fed on wild seeds and worms now nest in urban structures and eat scraps on the street. Peregrine falcons, also naturally cliff-nesters, in turn live on skyscrapers and feed on the pigeons! City parks offer some of the same nesting possibilities for wild birds but often with fewer predators to raid their nests. Raccoons find foraging in urban areas very rewarding and are often twice the size of their counterparts living deep in the forest. Animals get used to the sounds of traffic and having people nearby. This can get them into trouble sometimes if they are caught raiding garbage cans or wander into traffic.

As urban areas take up more space and forests dwindle, more and more wild animals may become adapted to life in the city.

# What Can Be Done

### Plant an Urban Garden

**Urban gardens are a great way to provide food and habitat to urban wildlife. Try these small gardens.**

1. Take a fork and a packet of flower seeds called alyssum. They come in white or pink. Use the fork to loosen the soil between cracks in the sidewalk (a less-used sidewalk is better). Sprinkle the seeds in the loosened soil. Water. Check on it later. They will bloom all summer.
2. Place a pot of soil on your windowsill. Plant flower seeds that birds and butterflies will like. Choose daisies, zinnias, bee balm, and fuchsias.
3. Place any hardy potted plant out on your fire escape or front step. String it with berries, popcorn, or small seeds rolled into suet. Watch the birds come visit!
4. Attract birds to a tree outside your window the same way. String it with berries, popcorn, or small seeds rolled into suet.

# City Critters

Take a pad and paper and go downtown to a city park. Sit on a bench and look around. What animals do you see? Birds? Squirrels? Write down everything you see. Take some time to really look and listen. Do you hear birds calling? Do you see insects of any kind around you? Bees? Butterflies? There are a lot more animals in urban habitats than you might have thought, right?

The EVERYTHING KIDS' Environment Book

# Chapter 3

# How We Affect the Environment

## Did You Know?

**Alligators Protect Game Fish**

Did you know that when the American alligator became endangered from over-hunting, all the fish started to disappear? That was because alligators eat a large fish called a gar, which feeds on many kinds of game fish. When the alligators disappeared, the gar populations exploded and they ate all the fish! Not until the alligator was protected and began to recover did the gar populations come under control so the other fish species could come back, too.

# Keystone Species

People don't always understand the interconnections in an ecosystem. If an animal is considered a particular pest, we often try to get rid of it. Sometimes this can upset whole ecosystems and make things a lot worse. This is especially true if the animal is a keystone species.

An example of people altering an entire ecosystem involved a little mammal on the California coast—the sea otter. They were hunted for their fur almost to extinction in the 1700–1800s. Then fishermen began to see changes in the ecosystem without the sea otter. Sea otters are one of the few animals that eat sea urchins. When the otters disappeared, the sea urchin population grew rapidly. Sea urchins, in turn, feed on kelp. The kelp beds are also very important to several fish populations as a place to spawn. So with the otters gone and the sea urchins on the rise, the kelp beds began to disappear too. Then the fish, having lost their spawning site, disappeared as well. Suddenly, in just a few years, the fishermen found that the fish were gone.

Then, in 1911, a treaty was passed that protected sea otters from hunting (the International Fur Seal Treaty). In the areas where sea otter numbers recovered, the sea urchin populations were brought back under control. Then the kelp beds recovered and the fish populations came back too. This is an example of how a keystone species is interconnected with a whole ecosystem.

# Habitat Loss Around the World

Habitat loss is a very serious problem on our planet today. All animals have a habitat in which they live, whether it's a vast rainforest or a tiny anthill. They have food to eat and a safe place to sleep and raise their young. They compete for food with other species and protect their habitat by being territorial or migrating from place to place to find more food. When humans

# Historic Garbage

Imagine that some litterbug has thrown a bag of trash on the side of the road. If no one stops to pick it up, some of that trash could still be there in a hundred years or more! See if you can match each item with the number of years it will take to decay (break down).

5 years

250 years

10-20 years

1 million years

200-500 years

30-40 years

# TryThis

## Save a Tree!

Try having a live Christmas tree this year. Instead of buying a cut tree, purchase a large potted evergreen. Or you can start the summer before and buy a balsam fir or blue spruce from a nursery and keep it in a large pot through the fall. Bring it inside before it gets too cold. Be sure and keep watering it all winter, since it won't be getting any rain indoors! Then dress it at Christmas time. It might be smaller than the trees you are used to having, but it will make the pile of presents look A LOT bigger. Then next summer, plant it in your yard!

# What Can Be Done

## Wildways for Wildlife

Many conservation groups have formed to try to protect and restore "wildways." These are wild areas from Canada to Mexico that are linked together to provide migration paths for birds and mammals. This is important to try and reduce the fragmentation of wild areas and the effect that has on wildlife. Migrating birds and mammals need safe wild areas to rest, feed, and travel through in the changing seasons.

clear a forest for farming or to build homes, whatever animals live in that forest lose their habitat. This is a very serious threat for animals that have limited habitat. It can lead to extinction.

As the human population expands, more and more natural habitats are destroyed to make way for the needs of humans. Fragmented habitats result, with some areas developed while others are left wild. The animals that survive may move into the smaller fragments of their habitat. This increases competition and stress in the remaining habitat. It can result in some species dying out. This decreases the biodiversity of the habitat.

## Panda Panic

An example of habitat loss affecting a species is the giant panda. Although protected from hunting and listed as an endangered species in 1984, panda numbers are still declining. This is because the giant panda feeds almost totally on bamboo, and the bamboo forests have been cut down to make way for the ever-expanding population of China. The pandas are left in small, isolated bamboo forests separated by development. When an area of bamboo has an occasional die-off, in which the bamboo all dies as a result of natural causes, the pandas can't get to another bamboo forest to feed. The giant panda is one of the most endangered mammals in the world. It is believed that there are less than 1,600 left. There is so little nutrition in bamboo that they have to eat for fourteen hours a day to get calories and cannot even stop eating to hibernate without starving! Unless the Chinese can stop development of panda habitat, it is just a matter of time before the pandas will be lost forever.

# Deforestation— The Disappearing Rainforest

Rainforests are disappearing very quickly. You read about it in the paper, see it on television, and learn about it in school. You might wonder if it's so bad, why do people keep doing it? We have talked about how people cut rainforests for the valuable timber or clear rainforest for farming. But there are other reasons as well. You might not like to hear this, but we, here in the United States, might be part of the reason. Here's how.

In Brazil the rapid slashing and burning of the rainforest is mostly for commercial use of the land—for cattle ranching. Brazil is one of the world's leading exporters of beef. The cattle that are raised there must be moved often, because the thin soil doesn't support their grazing for very long. When they need more grazing land, where do you think they get it? Yes, that's right, they cut and burn more rainforest. So how do we in the United States support the Amazon rainforest being cut down in Brazil? The answer is that the beef raised there is sold to fast food restaurants in the United States and Europe. One thing is for sure—Americans love fast food hamburgers!

## What Can Be Done

### Eat a Soy Burger!

Americans are big consumers of fast food, especially kids! But most fast foods are full of fat, excess calories, and cost a lot. The fast food industry also buys a lot of beef from Brazil where rainforests are being stripped to make room for more beef cattle. So next time you have a craving for fast food, have a soy burger instead. You never know, you might love them!

## Environmental Experiment

### Deforestation Frustration—Erosion

When forests are completely cut down, it removes all the protection from the soil. Serious erosion can result. Try this experiment to see what happens to the soil that's left behind. You will need an open soil area outside—a garden spot before any seeds are planted is perfect, some grass clippings, some dead twigs, a hose with a spray nozzle, and a gardening trowel (little shovel).

1. Loosen the soil with the trowel, and make three mounds a few inches high.
2. Leave the first mound as it is. It is an area cleared of trees completely.
3. Cover the second mound with grass clippings and stick in a few (3–4) broken twigs. This is an area that has been cut for timber selectively.
4. The third pile should get twig trees stuck into it thickly like a forest, then top it with a blanket of lawn clippings in between. This is an uncut forest.
5. Using the hose on the widest spray pattern (with the least water pressure), spray the three mounds evenly. Spray them until tiny streams of water are running down the unprotected mound. Turn off the water.
6. Examine the three mounds. How did they each fare under the hose's spray? Did the unprotected mound wash away with no vegetation to protect it? Did the timbered mound have less erosion than the unprotected mound? How did the forested mound do? Can you guess how a clear-cut forest would do in a big rainstorm?

# Environmental Experiment

## Desertification Education

Desertification is usually caused by poor agricultural practices compounded by drought. You can test this theory with a simple experiment. You will need a potted plant, another pot of soil about the same size as the plant (it should never have had a plant in it, just soil), a fan, some old newspapers, and a sunny spot by a window.

1. Set the two pots side by side in the window. Water them both the same amount. Then let them sit for a week with no water.
2. After a week (depending upon how sunny it is) they both should be pretty dry. Now you can water the plant, but NOT the soil. The plant represents how areas with vegetation have more active water cycle activities going on, so the planted habitat will get some rain. The empty pot is overgrazed terrain that is getting no rain activity.
3. After about a month of watering the plant once a week (and not watering the drought-stricken overgrazed region) you are ready to demonstrate the consequences of desertification.
4. Lay both pots on newspaper next to a wall. Make sure the newspaper comes up the side of the wall a bit to protect it.
5. Now turn on the fan facing the plants against the wall. Let the air blow on both pots. It can be a light breeze or a strong gusty wind.
6. What effect did the wind have on the two pots? Did the plant and moist soil protect the potted plant from losing as much soil as the empty, dry pot? This is a simplified look at the extreme consequences of desertification.

## Life After Deforestation

The effects of deforestation are sometimes surprising. It's sad to see a beautiful rainforest cut down and know the animals have lost their habitat, but these are not the only reasons to worry about deforestation. Rainforests play a part in our global environment. They house many different kinds of animals and plants, helping to preserve biodiversity. They play a role in the oxygen cycle, supplying badly needed oxygen to our atmosphere, while taking in all the carbon dioxide we make. They hold moisture in the atmosphere, acting like giant, green sponges. When you cut down a rainforest, you lose the protective cover of the trees and the bare ground is pounded by rain, losing its topsoil to erosion. Once gone, new soil can take generations to develop. Plus, what happens to the soil that gets washed away? It can cause other environmental problems. It washes downhill into rivers and builds up. This is called sedimentation. The river fills in and gets shallower. Boats then can't travel in the shallow waterways. The river can become murky, making fishing a lot harder. All of these things affect the lives of the people and animals in and around the rainforest. These are just some of the dramatic side effects of deforestation.

## Desertification

Sometimes the difference between a desert and a dry grassland is just a few inches of rain per year. The grasses hold the soil in place and the habitat, though dry, is relatively stable. With desertification this all changes. There are many reasons why a grassland turns into a desert, and the one you might think is the most obvious—a long drought—is actually rarely the reason! It is almost always due to the actions of humans that desertification changes a habitat.

# Transform a Tire

In 1989, only 10 percent of the scrap tires in the United States were reused. Thankfully, things have changed! To find out how many tires are now recycled, look at the pairs of tires below. Some look like they are linked through each other. Others look like two tires that overlap, but are not linked. Read the letters (from left to right, top to bottom) that are in the unlinked tires.

I love recycled tires!

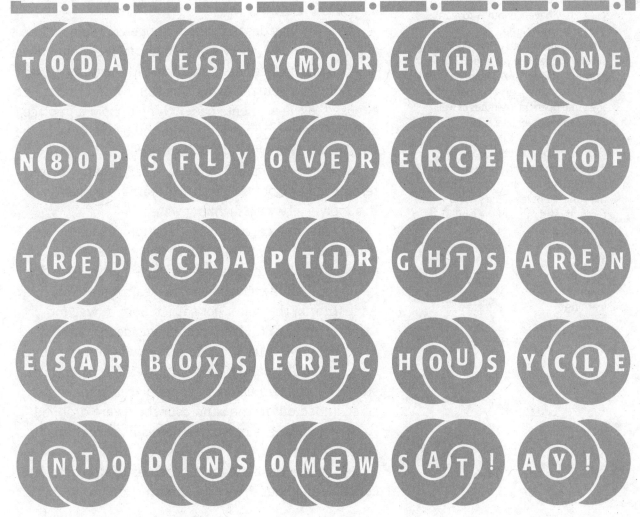

| T O D A | T E S T | Y M O R | E T H A | D O N E |
| N 8 0 P | S F L Y | O V E R | E R C E | N T O F |
| T R E D | S C R A | P T I R | G H T S | A R E N |
| E S A R | B O X S | E R E C | H O U S | Y C L E |
| I N T O | D I N S | O M E W | S A T ! | A Y ! |

# Environmental Experiment

## Noise Pollution and Learning

Can noise pollution keep you from learning? With a group of friends try this experiment. You will need two rooms, a pair of earplugs, two copies of a short poem (4 lines or less).

1. Choose two people as learners. They each get a copy of the poem to learn.
2. Put one person in a room with the door closed and earplugs in their ears. They have 5 minutes to learn the poem by heart.
3. The other person sits on the floor of the second room while you and a couple of friends talk and make noise around them. They have to try and memorize the same poem in 5 minutes as well. They cannot cover their ears.
4. At the end of 5 minutes bring both learners into one room. Have the noise victim try and recite the poem out loud from memory first. Then have the silent learner try. Who remembered more of the poem? What does this tell us about noise pollution and learning?

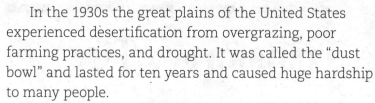

In the 1930s the great plains of the United States experienced desertification from overgrazing, poor farming practices, and drought. It was called the "dust bowl" and lasted for ten years and caused huge hardship to many people.

One big reason for desertification is overgrazing. A semi-arid grassland that is overgrazed by cattle loses the little protection it has. With no plant roots left to hold it in place, topsoil blows away in the wind or washes away in the next rain. The land becomes a desert. Twenty-four billion tons of topsoil are lost every year to erosion by wind, water, and other causes.

## Other Causes

Another way desertification happens is when a forest is completely cleared by slash-and-burn technique. This is when all the trees are cut down and then everything is set on fire to burn it away. The thin topsoil that is left exposed to the elements has nothing to hold it in place, and just like overgrazed land, the soil blows away in the wind or washes away in the next rain.

A river valley can turn into a desert when people reroute water from the river upstream for irrigation or to supply a city with drinking water.

An extreme case of desertification caused by irrigation happened in Russia with the Aral Sea. The rivers that fed into the sea were diverted to irrigate dry lands for farming. Over time the sea began to shrink. As it shrank, the water got saltier. Soon it was too salty for the fish to live. The sea was dead. Where it dried up, it left a flat, salt desert. Now when the wind blows, the salty sand blows out into the hills and ruins surrounding farm fields. In some places giant ships sit stranded out in the sand as if they were dropped from space. This is one extreme result of man-made desertification.

People are trying to take measures to stop desertification throughout the world. Limiting grazing animals in dry areas and planting trees or building sand fences to block winds helps to slow the process, but it will be a constant challenge to keep the desert from creeping into our drier lands.

## Noise Pollution

You might not think about noise as being pollution, but like air and water pollution, noise pollution can cause illness in humans and wildlife. Most loud noise throughout the world comes from types of transportation, like cars, trains, and planes. One car may not make a lot of noise, but think about a highway with thousands of cars moving along like a river of noise! Homes within 60 miles (100 km) of an airport are affected by the taxiing, takeoff, flyover, and landing noise of sometimes dozens of airplanes a day. People who live near railroad tracks can be startled by whistles and the rumbling of passing trains. Recreational vehicles, like ATVs, have increased noise pollution affecting people that live away from city traffic and seriously disturb wildlife. (Their role in trail erosion has also attracted national attention.) Other sources of noise include machines, power tools, office equipment, garden and lawn equipment, and even music.

## WORDS to KNOW

**SEMIARID:** Semi-arid describes habitats that are very dry, with scrubby plants and hardy animals, but are not considered deserts.

**IRRIGATION:** Irrigation is when water channels are created to bring in water to a dry area to grow crops.

### Did You Know?

**Cave Noise and Sleeping Bats**
Noise in a cave with hibernating bats can cause them to wake before there is food available (insects). This results in the bats using their fat reserves, which can cause them to starve to death before spring.

ENGINE 5.

# Reuse That Junk

**See how many useful items you can spell by using the letters in**

# N-E-W-S-P-A-P-E-R-S and J-U-N-K  M-A-I-L.

1. _____
2. _____
3. _____
4. _____
5. _____
6. _____
7. _____
8. _____
9. _____
10. _____
11. _____
12. _____
13. _____
14. _____
15. _____

## Reducing the Racket

Many towns and cities have noise rules and regulations and many things are being done to reduce the racket out there. Highway departments put up noise barriers between big highways and neighborhoods. These can be grassy hills, trees and other vegetation, or sometimes just a big, cement wall. Hopefully, over time, as more people use quiet hybrid cars, noise from traffic will go down. Hybrid cars are the first cars in 100 years that are actually lowering the noise pollution that cars make.

## Noise Can Make You Deaf

Noise pollution does not just hurt a person's hearing, though over time it can lead to permanent hearing loss. Noise can also add to stress, higher blood pressure, and even heart disease! It can make people mad and frustrated when they are woken from sleep or unable to concentrate. Noise near schools can affect children's ability to pay

The *EVERYTHING KIDS'* Environment Book

attention in class, learn new things, and concentrate on reading. Noise pollution can even frighten wildlife and interfere with their important behaviors like eating, mating, and migration.

# Light Pollution

Light pollution is a problem in many cities throughout the world. It comes from streetlights, building lights, outdoor lights, and advertising lights for stores and other businesses. From a distance you can see the glow of many cities in the night sky. This is called sky glow. Some cities give off so much light that they can be seen from space!

## The Danger of Too Much Light

Too much light can waste energy, but it also has an effect on people. Light, like sound, crosses boundaries and can frustrate neighbors, shining into their homes and keeping them awake at night. Glaring lights can blind drivers and cause accidents. Bright lights in the workplace all day long can lead to headaches, high blood pressure, and nervousness.

Too much light can make seeing stars harder. Astronomers and people who want to look at the stars must go to an area with less lighting to get a better look. Observatories are located in low-light areas and get regulations to keep the areas that way. For example, when the California Institute of Technology built its observatory on Palomar Mountain in the 1930s, the spot was chosen because it was so dark that the 200-inch telescope could see very faint, distant galaxies. But over the years southern California has become very built up and the lights of the cities cause sky glow in the night sky. The Palomar Observatory has tried to work with local governments to keep the light down so they can continue their important astronomy work.

**SKY GLOW:** Sky glow is the light glow in the night sky over cities. It makes viewing the night sky difficult.

# What a Racket!

**Noise pollution comes in many forms. Use the letters from N-O-I-S-E to fill in the blanks so you can read this silly story!**

J_mmy was pract_c_ng h_s v_ _l_n wh_l_ h_s dad was try_ _g t_ read th_ pap_r. Whe_ J_mmy w_uld play, th_ fam_ly d_g w_uld h_wl l_udly. F_ _ally h_s dad y_ll_d, "Ca_'t y_u play a tu_ _ that th_ d_g d_ _ _ _'t k_ _w?"

## Turn Out the Lights to See the Stars

You can easily test how light pollution affects what you can see in the night sky. On a clear night lie out in your backyard. Make sure all your outside lights are off and any inside lights that shine into the backyard. Let your eyes adjust until the night sky is clear. Look at all the stars and the details you can see. Now have someone turn on the outside light. Look at the stars now. Are they as clear as they were before? This is light pollution!

You can help prevent light pollution and save energy by turning off lights when you aren't using them, use lower watt bulbs if you don't need bright lights, and keep your lamps pointed to where you need the light to go.

## Our Light Affecting Wildlife

Our natural world has a night and day cycle that animals have adapted to over millions of years. With light pollution making even the nighttime bright in some places, the life patterns of wildlife can get disturbed. All you have to do is see a mob of insects crowding around your porch light at night to see how bright light confuses animals and can distract them from their normal life patterns.

The *EVERYTHING KIDS* Environment Book

# Invasive Species

When a foreign species is introduced to an ecosystem, it can upset a balance that has been in the works for a long time. Many native species have been driven near to extinction by these invaders taking over. Sometimes it takes a long time for people to realize that an alien species is having an effect on native wildlife and by then the species is so well established that getting rid of it is impossible.

There are hundreds of invasive species that have been introduced into the United States over time. These include fire ants, the Asian long-horned beetle, Africanized honeybees, ladybugs, gypsy moths, starlings, and many more. It is a costly and difficult problem to get rid of invasive species once they get into an ecosystem.

In 1884, at an ornamental plant exposition in New Orleans, American gardeners got their first glimpse of the beautiful purple flowers of the water hyacinth, a native plant of South America. A Florida gardener took a cutting back home and dropped it into his garden pond. Within weeks the water hyacinth had taken over the pond. To get rid of it, he pitched it into the St. Johns River. This began a century-long battle to get this aggressive plant back under control.

The water hyacinth grows at an amazing rate, spreading floating mats of vegetation so thick that it blocks light to the underwater environment, killing lakes and ponds. People tried to chop it up and then burn it, only to find that each small piece started a new plant! They brought in manatees to graze on the plants but they grew so fast up rivers and canals that within a few years they had spread to several southern states. Finally in the 1960s, people started spraying the water hyacinth with herbicides. Herbicide, a strong, toxic substance that poisons plants, did kill the water hyacinth, but it also meant that the poison got into rivers and lakes.

## Did You Know?

### A Speedy Weed

Kudzu, an invasive vine from Japan, was imported because it grew fast and was a good groundcover that helped stop erosion. Soon it grew over whole forests blocking sunlight until all the trees died. It grew over barns, houses, fences, and power lines. Controlling it has not been easy. The most effective control found so far is grazing goats!

Some invasive species have a worse effect than others. Sailors brought dogs and pigs to the small, isolated island of Maurituis, off the coast of Africa, leading to the downfall of the flightless dodo, whose ground nests were plundered by these non-native predators. Weasels and cats brought to New Zealand also devastated the ground-nesting and flightless birds living there. Goats introduced to the Galapagos Islands have stripped vegetation clean. Many countries now have rules about bringing any plants or animals across their borders. They have learned some hard and expensive lessons from past introductions.

# Chapter 4
# The Air and Water

# Environmental Experiment

## Is It Hot in Here?

How would the greenhouse effect warm up Earth's climate? Try this experiment to see. You will need two jars, two inexpensive, metal-cased thermometers, two dark washcloths, a paper and pencil to record results, one lid, and a sunny window.

1. Put a dark washcloth inside each jar. Lay the jars on their sides in the sunny window.
2. Lay one thermometer inside each jar facing up so you can read it.
3. Put a lid on one jar. Leave the other one open.
4. Watch the thermometers closely for 20 minutes. Check the temperatures every 2 minutes and record the time and temperatures.
5. After 20 minutes open the jars and remove the thermometers.
6. What difference did you notice in the temperatures between the two jars?
7. Explain what you see.

# Climate Change

Our atmosphere keeps the earth's temperature stable. It lets just the right amount of sunlight through so the earth doesn't get too hot in the summer. It also keeps warmth from escaping so we don't get too cold in the winter. In this way the atmosphere acts like a greenhouse. This is called the "greenhouse effect." It is part of what makes our planet the comfortable place that it is.

Lately scientists have been worried that too many "greenhouse gases" are building up in our atmosphere. Humans are driving more cars and heating more homes than ever before. We do this mostly by burning fossil fuels (oil and gasoline) and coal. This burning releases greenhouse gases, like carbon dioxide, into the atmosphere. At the same time we are cutting down trees in record numbers. Trees help take up carbon dioxide in the atmosphere and replace it with the oxygen we need. Scientists worry that if we have fewer trees *and* make more carbon dioxide, we will build up greenhouse gases faster than ever before. This might block even more heat from escaping into space, and like a greenhouse with its windows shut on a hot, sunny day, it might be getting a bit warmer on Earth. This warming effect is called global warming.

## Turning Up the Heat

The rise in Earth's temperatures might be just a few degrees, but over time it could have a big effect. Scientists worry that it will eventually cause the polar ice caps to melt and the sea levels to rise. This could change weather patterns and alter habitats in a way that might result in many animals going extinct. It's still early to know all the effects of global warming on our planet, but it's important to know how our actions can make a difference.

## Melting Polar Ice Caps

NASA studies Earth from space via satellites. From here they can see changes in the shape and size of the polar ice caps. They can see that the year-round ice pack in the Arctic is shrinking. In the past twenty-five years it has shrunk 10 percent. Scientists have also been watching satellites that have been collecting the earth's surface temperatures for twenty years. They show that the temperatures are rising. In 2003 the largest ice shelf in the Arctic that had been in place for 3,000 years, broke up into the ocean. Climate does change naturally over time, but rapid changes are unusual. These facts may signal global warming.

How would melting ice caps affect the planet? For one thing, the bright white ice caps reflect a lot of the sun's energy back into space. As the ice caps shrink, more sunlight will be absorbed by the earth, warming the climate even more. Melting ice caps would make more water available for the water cycle, which could change the rain patterns and how salty the ocean is around the poles, affecting ocean fisheries.

The shrinking ice shelf is already affecting arctic animal populations. Species like polar bear who hunt seals off ice shelves are unable to find prey as easily without the frozen platforms. Scientists have found that hungry polar bears are drowning while trying to get to prey without the usual ice shelves available to hunt from.

## Pollution at Sea

Ocean pollution can come in many forms. It can result from oil tankers spilling oil, boats sinking, or even ocean litter. Large or small, ocean debris can cause problems for both sea life and humans. Garbage gets into the ocean when people dump it off boats and litter beaches, but it also can reach the ocean from rivers, storm drains, or ocean dumping of industrial waste. Eventually all water on land flows toward the sea.

Besides being ugly to look at, a lot of ocean debris, like plastic bottles, bags, Styrofoam peanuts, old fishing wire, and nets are quite dangerous to wildlife. Whales

## WORDS to KNOW

**GREENHOUSE GASES:** Greenhouse gases include water vapor, carbon dioxide, methane, nitrous oxide, and ozone; too much of these in our atmosphere leads to increased warming, as in a greenhouse.

# TryThis

### Melt Some Ice Caps

**Will the melting ice caps dilute the ocean's salt water around them? Will it raise the ocean levels? To test this you will need two clear glasses, some ice, and a dark liquid.**

1. Fill both glasses halfway with a dark liquid, like grape juice or cola.
2. Then fill the rest of one glass with ice.
3. Leave them both on the counter until all the ice is melted.
4. Look at both glasses. What do you notice? The glass with the melted ice is fuller, the water level rose. The dark liquid is also lighter. It is diluted. If that liquid had been salt water like the ocean, it would be less salty now!

### Did You Know?

#### Gas Spills at Home

More gas is spilled every year when people fill up their lawnmowers, weed trimmers, and chippers than was spilled in the whole *Exxon Valdez* oil spill.

and dolphins eat plastic bags thinking they are squid, sea turtles and ocean birds eat Styrofoam peanuts that block their digestive tracts, and abandoned fishing nets tangle and drown thousands of seals every year. Even human swimmers and divers can get tangled in dumped nets and drown.

Other dangerous ocean pollutants include human sewage, oil spilled at sea, and medical waste dumped in the ocean. These hazards endanger both ocean animals and human swimmers and wash up on our beaches. Fish and shellfish become so toxic from eating pollutants that they are not safe for people to catch and eat either. This affects lobstermen and fishermen's livelihoods.

### An Oily Mess

Despite all efforts, sometimes spills happen. On March 24, 1989, the *Exxon Valdez*, a huge oil tanker, hit a reef in Prince William Sound in Alaska. The hull of the ship cracked open and spilled more than 11 million gallons of crude oil into the sound. That oil spill was the largest in U.S. history. A spill that large is very bad anywhere, but a spill in Prince William Sound was even harder to deal with because there was so much wildlife to save and clean up. Afterward, Congress passed the Oil Pollution Act of 1990. It made stricter rules for oil tankers, their owners, and captains. The tankers have to have stronger hulls and ship captains have to be in better contact with vessel traffic centers. No one wants a spill like that to happen ever again.

## Over-Fishing the Oceans

People used to think that the ocean had an unlimited source of fish. After all, the oceans cover three-fourths of the earth's surface. For thousands of years people have gotten their food and livelihood from the sea. Lately, however, we have come to realize that some ocean animals are disappearing. This has happened because of years of over-fishing. Over-fishing is when fishermen take more fish than can be replaced by new fish eggs being hatched. Fish populations can also be hurt by increased ocean pollution.

## Who's Keeping Track of All the Fish?

The U.S. Fisheries Department keeps track of fishery levels in the oceans. The fish that people most like to eat (so fisherman most like to catch) are cod, haddock, and blue-finned tuna. These are the fish that have become the most endangered from over-fishing. The U.S. Fisheries department rates populations of fish from abundant to depleted. All three of these most popular fish plus many others are rated as depleted. They have become the most endangered.

It is hard to make fishermen stop fishing when fishing is the job they have always done. It also may be one of the few good jobs on an island or in a coastal village, and people have to feed their families. Plus no one owns the ocean. Anyone in the world can move around on the ocean and fish where they please. For these reasons, it is

# What Can Be Done

### Restoring Ocean Ecosystems

**Fisheries experts have suggested many ways to help, including:**

1. Limit the number of fish that can be caught at any time.
2. Only let fishing boats fish a few days per month.
3. Make some parts of the ocean no-fishing zones while fisheries recover and then rotate which country can fish there at which time of year.
4. Buy out older boats from fishermen, so they will retire or move on to other jobs.
5. Make nets with bigger mesh so baby fish can escape, grow up, and make more baby fish!
6. Keep track of fishing boat activities by satellite.

# TryThis

### Clean Up Your Own Oil Spill

**How hard is it to clean up an oil spill at sea? Try this simple activity to see. You will need some dark-colored olive oil, a pie or cake pan, a feather, some of your dog's fur (brush it off, don't cut it off!), some dishwashing soap, and a spoon.**

1. Fill a cake pan half full with water. Drip in some olive oil. You have created an oil spill!
2. What happens to animals that swim through an oil spill at sea or walk through an oil spill on the beach? Drag the feather and then the dog fur through the oil. What happens? It sticks. Can you imagine how hard it would be to clean off thousands of birds and mammals?
3. Shake the cake pan gently to create wave action. See how the oil breaks up and spreads around. It still doesn't mix with the water, but it spreads. This is why oil cleanup in the ocean has to happen fast.
4. Try to scrape the oil out of the water with a spoon. It's very hard to get it all, isn't it?
5. Try some other cleanup materials like paper towels, cotton, or a square of cloth. How do these work?
6. Now add more oil in the center of the pan again till you have a little pool (about a tablespoon). Now drip a couple of drops of dishwashing soap right into the center of the oil. What happens? What happens when you shake the pan gently? Isn't it surprising how well the soap dissolves the oil? Soap is a strong solvent. So why don't they just dump lots of liquid soap on oil spills? Would you want soap in your drinking water? How would soap affect all the sea animals? Would it be even worse than oil? Aren't you glad you didn't have a real oil spill to deal with?

# Message in a Bottle

Use a light-colored marker to connect the letters.

Begin in the square below the word *START*.

Follow the arrows.

If a square has no arrow, keep going in the same direction until you find the next arrow.

*Extra Fun:* Read the unused letters

START

The EVERYTHING KIDS' Environment Book

not easy to get people to stop fishing for long enough to let the fisheries recover.

### Growing Ocean Fish on Land

Many countries have begun to grow their own ocean fish in saltwater fisheries. This may help relieve the pressure on the depleted ocean fisheries. But to really save our ocean fisheries, people will have to fish only at rates that would give fish populations time to recover.

## Our Ailing Coral Reefs

Coral reefs sit along the shores of many tropical places. These are areas that are constantly churned by the waves moving back and forth at shoreline. Coral reefs benefit from coastal wave action because the waves shower them with bits of food over and over. The waves also stir up oxygen over the reefs that the animals there need to survive. Lastly, the waves keep sand from building up on the coral anchored there. Coral are animals and cannot survive if they are buried in sand.

Coral reefs have amazing biodiversity, with a huge assortment of animals and plants living among them. The salty, warm environment (between 68° and 82°F) keeps the reefs healthy and thriving.

### The Partnership Between Algae and Coral

Coral reefs have a partnership with algae called zooxanthellae. Zooxanthellae algae lives in the coral tissue itself. It helps the coral by providing food and oxygen while taking up the carbon dioxide the coral releases. For the algae, it is a safe place to live and grow. Zooxanthellae algae is what gives coral its many pretty colors. It is very sensitive. If the coral reef becomes polluted or the water temperature changes, the zooxanthellae algae will die and the coral loses its pretty colors. This is called coral bleaching and is a sign of an unhealthy coral reef.

# TryThis

## Create a Flood

**How do wetlands protect towns from flooding? To test this you will need 2 pie or cake pans, a ¼ cup measuring cup, a damp sponge, and some water.**

1. Lay the two pans next to each other. Wring out the sponge so that it has no excess water. Then place it in the center of one of the pans.
2. Pour ¼ cup water into the empty pan. Notice how it covers the bottom of the pan. Now pour a ¼ cup water into the second pan right onto the sponge.
3. What is the difference in the water level of the pans? Imagine that these pans are each small valleys with tiny towns. The pan without the sponge would be underwater. How would the town with the sponge fare? Towns with wetlands are like the pan with the sponge. Wetlands take on and hold excess water in a storm and release it slowly without flooding.

## The Attack on Coral Reefs

Coral reefs are always under pressure from collectors, who harvest the colorful corals and fish for aquariums and other markets. Snorkeling tourists walk on the fragile plants and animals and boaters pollute the delicately balanced habitat. Coral reefs are one of our most biologically diverse habitats, but they are also very delicate and are in serious danger. In 1998 President Clinton helped establish the U.S. Coral Reef Task Force to better preserve and protect coral reef ecosystems.

# The Importance of Wetlands

People used to think that wetlands were wasted land. Developers would drain them with ditches, fill them in with tons of soil, and build houses, schools, and parking areas on them. Then scientists began to realize the important role wetlands played in the environment.

Wetlands act like giant sponges during storms. They soak up extra storm water and afterward release it slowly back into the water cycle. This helps prevent flooding. Towns where people have drained wetlands have found that in a big storm, their streets and homes are often flooded because there are no wetlands to soak up the excess water.

Wetlands also act as giant filters where pollutants are absorbed and dissolved over time. Though wetlands can become polluted from dumping, wastewater, and fertilizer runoff from farm fields, they are able to process some pollutants over time because of all the microorganisms and plants living there.

Wetlands are especially important for providing homes and breeding grounds to millions of birds, fish, and amphibians worldwide. Many wetlands have become national wildlife refuges, where you can go to take pictures and look at birds and animals.

The **EVERYTHING KIDS** Environment Book

## The Everglades

The Everglades are a huge wetland that once covered more than four million acres of southern Florida. Sometimes called the "river of grass," the Everglades are a shallow sheet of water that slowly flowed across a grassy plain. In the late 1800s people began draining parts of the Everglades for development. Roads were built and towns sprang up. The Everglades shrank to half its original size. Cities like Miami grew up where once there was a thriving wetland. Sewage and waste from the cities were pumped into the remaining wetlands. Over time scientists began to see the importance of the Everglades. Even with its smaller size, the Everglades filtered the pollutants coming from the cities, absorbing the worst of it like a sewage treatment plant. During storms the Everglades protected the cities from storm surge flooding. They also are just a great place to visit and see wildlife.

### Did You Know?

**Pollution and Breathing**

People in areas of high air pollution can develop breathing problems, especially kids! The World Health Organization has estimated that more than four million people die each year from air pollution.

# Much Too Much!

Use the decoder to figure out how one student took recycling a little too far!

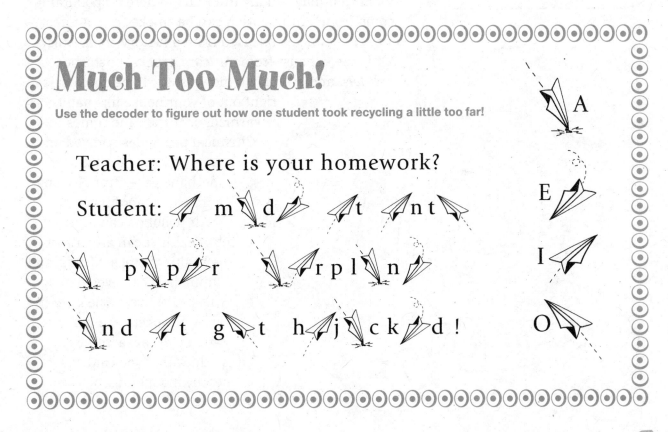

Teacher: Where is your homework?

Student: I made it into a paper airplane and it got hijacked!

A

E

I

O

# TryThis

## Is That Building Melting?

**Over decades acid rain can actually corrode buildings and statues. Try this experiment to see how this happens.**

1. Fill one glass bowl with water.
2. Fill one glass bowl with vinegar.
3. Add a piece of chalk (the same size) to each bowl and leave them over night. Chalk is made from a similar mineral that some buildings are made of—limestone.
4. In the morning take out both chalk pieces. Are they still the same size?
5. Over a long period of time acid rain corrodes buildings the way the vinegar corroded the chalk.

Now there is a big effort to protect what is left of the Everglades. Thousands of acres of man-made treatment marshes have been planted between the cities and the Everglades. They use native plants to naturally clean harmful nutrients from water flowing into the Everglades. Farmers have had to change their use of pesticides and fertilizers to avoid it reaching the Everglades. Hopefully over time, the Everglades' many endangered animals will begin to thrive again and this unique and beneficial wetland can be preserved for all time.

## Save Your Breath—Air Pollution

Though you may not notice it, the air around you holds many things besides the mixture of gases you breathe. It holds water vapor, dust, pollen, and sometimes—pollutants. Pollutants are things that are in our environment that may be harmful to us. Where do pollutants come from? Air pollution can be smoke from a forest fire or chemicals released from a factory smokestack. It is the exhaust from our cars, trucks, boats, buses, planes, and even lawn mowers! It can be chemicals right out of your house like paint, varnish, or turpentine fumes. Chemical pesticides sprayed on crops pollute the air. So do methane gases from rotting garbage in landfills.

Air pollution can affect your health. It can also affect the health of crops, forests, and animals. It can even damage the protective ozone layer in our atmosphere. Air pollution can make a haze in the sky so thick that you cannot see nearby mountains.

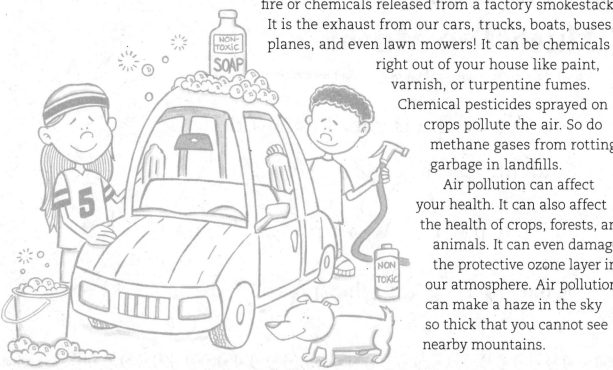

The EVERYTHING KIDS' Environment Book

### "Natural" Pollution

Not all pollution is man-made. Sometimes natural events can cause air pollution, like a volcano erupting, natural gas—like radon escaping into the air—or a lightning strike setting off a forest fire. Even dust blown off dry land can be an air pollution hazard. All these things are natural to our environment but still make air pollution that can harm us.

## Acid Rain—Our Struggling Lakes and Forests

Rain might seem like the cleanest source of water on Earth—after all, the only place it has been is in the clouds. However, rain and snow are affected by what they pass through on their way to the ground. Some factories release nitrogen and sulfur from their smokestacks. This mixes with falling rainwater and forms weak nitric and sulfuric acids. Then the rain (or snow) carries the acid to the ground, into lakes, streams, and forests. It changes the pH, making the soil and water more acidic than they would be naturally. Scientists call this acid rain. Acid rain can make the soil too acid for some plants to grow and slow the growth of trees. In lakes and streams it can make the water environment too acid for fish, frog, and salamander eggs to hatch. If lakes and ponds become acid enough they will eventually become completely lifeless.

### Don't Lower Your pH

Acidity is measured on a pH scale. Something with a pH of 1 is the most acid and something with a pH of 14 the most base (or alkaline). Pure water is considered to be neutral (it has a pH of 7). Normal rainwater has a pH of about 6. That is a little acidic. That is because even pure rainwater falls through carbon dioxide in the air. Rain with a pH of less than about 5.3 is considered acid rain. Rain in the northeastern states has a pH between 4 and 5. This is serious acid rain.

## Environmental Experiment

### Thirsty for Acid?

**How does acid rain affect plants? Try this experiment to see.**

1. Plant 3 bean seeds in three separate pots, place them in the window and let them grow. When all three plants are about 4 inches high they are ready to be tested.
2. Label the plants 1 to 3.
3. Always water #1 with ½ cup fresh water.
4. Always water #2 with ½ cup fresh water mixed with 1 teaspoon of vinegar.
5. Always water #3 with ½ cup fresh water mixed with 2 tablespoons of vinegar.
6. After a week can you see a difference in how the plants look? How about after two weeks? Write down the effects of the weak acid and strong acid treatments.
7. This is what acid rain does to plants. It weakens them and in some cases can kill them.

## The Answer Is Blowing in the Wind

In the United States acid rain is having its worst effect in the northeastern states. Some lakes in the Adirondack Mountains in upstate New York have gotten so acidic that fish and frog populations have begun to disappear. Acid rain even makes buildings and statues begin to corrode over time. Why is acid rain so bad in this area, when it has so few smokestacks of its own? There are three main reasons. One reason is the weather. The main winds in the United States blow from west to east. The second reason is where the pollution is made. Smokestacks in the industrial cities in the Great Lakes region of the United States and Canada belch out a lot of pollutants. The third reason is that to try and decrease local air pollution, the factories made their smokestacks taller. This pushed the pollution higher up in the atmosphere and it blew away in the strong winds. This made the local people much happier. The only problem was that it blew the pollutants right into the northeastern states.

In 1990, the U.S. Congress passed laws as part of the Clean Air Act to lower acid rain pollutants. Over time scientists hope that the decrease in sulfur and carbon emissions from factories will slow acid rain effects in the Northeast.

# Keep the Soap

Water pollution comes in many forms! Break the Vowel Switch Code to learn what one silly kid wants to do about it.

MIM: WHUT CUN WA DI TI STIP PILLOTENG IOR WUTAR?

SMALLY KED: HIW ABIOT E STIP TUKENG BUTHS?

## What Can Be Done

### Don't Support Poaching

**There are many ways you and your family help stop poaching.**

1. Never buy, sell, or own anything made from ivory. Even ivory that has been gotten legally drives the sale of, and even indirectly the poaching of, ivory. Remember, all ivory represents the death of an elephant or walrus.
2. Don't support coral reef poachers. Never buy coral for your fish tank unless it has been stamped with the Marine Aquarium Council (MAC). This makes sure the coral was raised for aquariums and not from a wild reef.
3. Don't keep exotic animal pets, even if you see them at the pet store. The exotic animal pet trade, though legal if regulated in the United States, is not regulated in all countries around the world. So owning exotic animals does drive the hunting of exotic species. It's best to leave wild animals in their natural habitat.
4. Spread the word!

## Loss of Biodiversity

Biodiversity is not just how much wildlife there is, but the different kinds of wildlife. Each different habitat, from rainforests to polar regions, has a variety of animals, plants, fungi, etc. Why is biodiversity so important? Every organism in an ecosystem plays some role in keeping things healthy and in balance. The overlapping jobs of organisms act as backup in case of drought, disease, flood, or fire. This complex tapestry of life has evolved over a long period of time. Even the smallest microbe in the soil plays its part. When species begin to disappear from an ecosystem, things balance on a much less secure foothold.

### An Ear for Trouble

An example of the danger in losing species variety can be shown with modern corn. American farmers over many generations bred the best-tasting sweet corn and planted only that pure strain year after year. This is called monoculture. Then a disease called corn smut attacked the crop. The corn had been bred to be so specific that it had little resistance to the fungus. The entire corn crop was destroyed. Agricultural researchers went to Mexico and searched out the wild maize that corn was descended from to find the gene that resisted smut and bred it back into the corn. Now farmers plant a variety of crops and strains to avoid the danger of crops losing their healthy biodiversity.

## Getting Our Endangered Species Act Together

Passed in 1973, the Endangered Species Act is meant to protect threatened and endangered plants and animals from going extinct. It also is meant to protect the habitats where endangered species are found. The numbers of plants and animals on the list changes, as studies show how the populations of plants and animals are

# Close to Home

Kids go to the zoo to see wild animals. But there is a lot of wildlife right in our backyards! We need to protect these creatures and save them some space, too. See if you can put the letter groups in the margin together to spell some common animal neighbors. Each word has been broken into three parts, and the first letters are given.
Hint: The pictures are clues!

S _ _ _ _ _ _

S _ _ _ _ _ _

S _ _ _ _ _ _ _ _

P _ _ _ _ _ _

R _ _ _ _ _ _

F _ _ _

C _ _ _ _ _ _ _ _ _

B _ _ _ _ _ _ _ _

M _ _ _ _

# Modern Motto

If we all learn to use less energy, land, and resources, there will be more of these treasures for everyone. Start by recycling these scrambled letters into familiar words! The definitions will give you a hint. When you are done, use the numbered letters in the shaded boxes to complete the saying below. To create a new look, use fabric paint to put this saying on an old T-shirt!

**Place to hang curtains**

NIOWWD

_ _ _ _ _ _
  2   10 14

**Slow moving creature with a hard shell**

LUTRTE

_ _ _ _ _ _
  7   13

**Opposite of south**

TRONH

_ _ _ _ _
  11  15

**Tool for gathering leaves**

EARK

_ _ _ _
 8 9

**Wiggly creature that lives in dirt**

MOWR

_ _ _ _
4 5

**Soft shoe worn at bedtime**

RPLSIPE

_ _ _ _ _ _ _
1     3

U _ E _ _ T _ U _ ,
  1    2     3

_ E A _ I _ O T ,
4   5   6   7

M _ _ E IT _ O ,
  8 9      10

OR D _ _ IH U _
     11   12   13   14   15

**Covered with liquid**

ETW

_ _ _
12  6

The EVERYTHING KIDS' Environment Book

doing. If an animal like the bald eagle recovers, it is taken off the endangered animal list and moved to a threatened animal list. If an animal like the Bactrian camel becomes so scarce that it is threatened with extinction, it is added to the endangered animal list.

## Why Do Things Become Endangered?

Most species become endangered because of loss of habitat. If an animal has no place to live, it will go extinct. So the Endangered Species Act gave the U.S. Fish and Wildlife Service (FWS) and the National Oceanic and Atmospheric Administration (NOAA) the job of picking habitats in specific locations on land or in U.S. coastal waters that needed protection to save the endangered species.

There are about 1,880 species listed under the Endangered Species Act. Only about 1,310 of them are actually found in the United States and its coastal waters. The rest are found in other countries. Some of our most endangered species on Earth include:

- Black-footed ferret
- California condor
- Giant panda
- Ibex
- Mountain gorilla
- Orangutan
- Snow leopard
- Sumatran rhino
- White rhinoceros
- Yangtze dolphin

To see the full list, go to: *www.fws.gov/endangered/ wildlife.html#Species*.

## Some Success with Endangered Species

The peregrine falcon was once very close to extinction because of the use of the pesticide DDT. The chemical was sprayed in wetlands to kill mosquitoes but moved up

**WORDS to KNOW**

**ENDANGERED:** A species is considered endangered if there are so few of them that they may soon become extinct.

# What Can Be Done

## Keeping the Endangered from Becoming Extinct

There are many animals that are close to extinction from habitat loss. The giant panda, tiger, snow leopard, and mountain gorilla are among them. What can be done to save them from extinction?

1. Protect the habitats in which they live.
2. Ban hunting and guard against poaching.
3. Ban any products made from them.
4. Make people aware so they know not to buy products made from these animals and will want to save them.

**TREATY:** A treaty is a signed agreement between two or more countries.

through the food chain as birds ate the insects and falcons ate the birds. DDT didn't kill the falcons outright but caused their eggs to have soft shells and break, so no new young could be born. Once scientists discovered what DDT did in the food chain, the chemical was banned and slowly animal populations began to recover. With a lot of help from wildlife biologists and a captive breeding program, peregrine falcon numbers have recovered. Now it is not unusual to see these amazing predators nesting on skyscrapers in New York City, hunting pigeons!

## Poaching

Most countries throughout the world have made laws to stop or limit hunting of endangered species. A treaty called the Convention on International Trade in Endangered Species of Wild Fauna and Flora (CITES) has been signed by most countries. Though many animals are protected from hunting, it does not stop some people from hunting them illegally. This is called poaching. Poaching happens all over the world, because poachers can get a lot of money for their illegal game. They sell the horns, ivory, body parts, and skin of protected animals. Even with game wardens hired to patrol animal preserves, poachers have the advantage. For one thing, preserves are very large tracts of land and there are not enough wardens to protect the whole area. The other problem is that poachers after big game like elephants and rhinos are armed and can be very dangerous. One warden may not be able to even try to stop six poachers. In many places poachers seem to be winning out over our vanishing species.

### Poaching Here at Home

Poaching does not just happen in Africa or Asia. There is a lot of poaching in our own National Parks right here in the United States! People steal cactuses, trees, tortoises, and even grass if they can sell it. It's a

The EVERYTHING KIDS' Environment Book

frustrating problem for those of us who want to protect our disappearing national treasures.

## How Animals Go Extinct

It is a natural part of an ecosystem that some animals adapt better than others. Over time they can squeeze the less adapted species out of their position to extinction. In studying man and the environment, it is easy to think that humans have caused all the extinctions of animals so far in the world, but in fact most extinctions happened millions of years ago before humans even lived on the planet! We know from the fossil record that thousands of prehistoric species of animals and plants have lived on Earth and over time have gone extinct, including all the dinosaurs.

### Ways We Drive Animals to Extinction

It is true that people have, through over-hunting, development, habitat destruction, and careless introduction of predators, caused many animals to go extinct. There are many examples of this to look at.

Often big mammals were hunted to "protect" people and their livestock. This happened to the Caspian tiger. Found across the Middle East, around the south end of the Caspian Sea and across into Asia, this tiger was driven to extinction by the Russian army. They were ordered to kill all the tigers to open up the region to development. Once the tigers were gone, towns grew up and the whole region became more developed and less "wild."

The most famous extinction, though, happened from the careless introduction of predators to a protected ecosystem. When sailors first landed on the island of Mauritius, off the coast of Africa, the large flightless birds living there—dodos—had never seen predators before. Sailors killed a lot of them right off for food and sport, but the biggest toll came from the new predators that arrived with the sailors on their ships. Dogs, cats, pigs, and rats preyed on the clueless dodos, as well as their

### Butterfly Gardens

Butterflies feed on the flower nectar of certain plants. You can plant these plants in your garden and attract a lot of visiting butterflies. You can also plant some flowers that their caterpillars like to eat. The butterflies will lay their eggs on those plants. Some examples of flowers that butterflies like are cosmos, Queen Anne's lace, zinnia, butterfly weed, coneflowers, New England asters, spearmint, milkweed, yarrow, phlox, and daylilies. These will also make beautiful gardens!

**FOSSIL RECORD:** Fossils are impressions of organisms that lived a long time ago that have been preserved in the rocks. The fossil record shows us when species went extinct relative to the passage of millions of years.

eggs and young in nests on the ground. It took less than 100 years for all of the dodos to disappear completely.

Even if the extinction of an animal is blamed on over-hunting, habitat loss is usually part of the story. Less than 200 years ago, there were grizzly bears that lived out on the American prairie. The plains grizzly was a fearsome sight to early settlers. Yet even these giant animals lost their habitat to the droves of new settlers invading the west and soon disappeared. Now plains grizzlies can only be found in some wild prairies in Northern Canada where few people live to disturb them.

Many species balance on the edge of extinction from habitat loss and may not last another generation. These include some of our favorite animals like the panda, orangutan, tiger, snow leopard, and mountain gorilla.

## Too Late for Some...

Our present-day awareness of the importance of protecting endangered species and their habitats is a good thing, but it has come too late for many species that have gone extinct throughout the world. Some have gone extinct not too long ago. Species like the passenger pigeon, Steller's sea cow, dodo, moa, and quagga all have disappeared in the last 400 years. There are many endangered animals that are being watched and taken care of in hopes of a return to safe numbers.

Hopefully, knowing the importance of healthy habitats and learning from the experiences with keystone species we can keep new animal extinctions down to the fewest number possible.

## Creating Animal Habitats

Animals need as much habitat as they can get to be successful. Usually all you hear about is people destroying habitat. You rarely hear about people making new animal habitats. The truth is it doesn't happen very often and when it does, it is usually by accident. What a great accident!

The EVERYTHING KIDS Environment Book

One unexpected kind of animal habitat that we have created are in landfills and garbage dumps. They may be gross, but they provide food and shelter for many mammals, birds, and insects. It is thought that the grizzly bears in Yellowstone Park would have gone extinct if it hadn't been for the garbage dumps there in the 1950s–60s. The same goes for sewers and subway systems, cow barns, agricultural fields, and orchards. Many man-made places provide alternate habitats to adaptive animals.

On a more pleasant note, flower gardens also create habitat for nectar-feeding animals like butterflies and hummingbirds. Vegetable gardens can house slugs, snails, snakes, rabbits, and beetles. One thing is for sure, humans do affect habitats with our presence.

### Welcome to the Bat Cave

Another example of humans creating a habitat happened in upstate New York. In that region there are very few natural caves, so the one animal that needs cave habitat to survive the winter—bats—were never very numerous in the state. Then in the late 1800s people started mining for ore in the Adirondack Mountains, in upstate New York. For many years, men dug miles and miles of underground mines and extracted ore. When the mining ended, they left miles of what were essentially—caves. In the last century, seven species of bats have made a foothold in upstate New York. All of them are small, insect-eating bats. The old mines act as perfect winter hibernation caves. The air temperature stays at about 50 degrees all winter so the bats can sleep safely and emerge in the spring to hunt for insects. The Adirondacks can be very buggy in the spring. The advantage for the people near the bat caves is that these bats can eat up to 500 mosquitoes an hour!

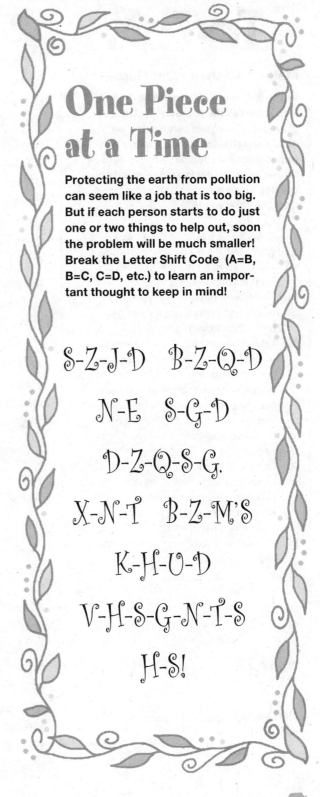

## One Piece at a Time

Protecting the earth from pollution can seem like a job that is too big. But if each person starts to do just one or two things to help out, soon the problem will be much smaller! Break the Letter Shift Code (A=B, B=C, C=D, etc.) to learn an important thought to keep in mind!

S-Z-J-D   B-Z-Q-D

N-E   S-G-D

D-Z-Q-S-G.

X-N-T   B-Z-M'S

K-H-U-D

V-H-S-G-N-T-S

H-S!

# TryThis

## Make Your Own Plant Guide

Be the only one in your neighborhood who knows all the names of the trees on the block. Make your own guide. You'll need a few sheets of white paper, a soft-tipped pencil or charcoal, a heavy book, a three-ringed binder (an old recycled one will do), a hole puncher, and a tree guide from the library.

1. Collect one leaf from each tree in your yard. If it is an evergreen collect a small stem with a few needles or bundles of needles on them.
2. Place them between two pieces of paper and press them flat under a heavy book overnight.
3. Take your newly flattened leaves out and lay each under a piece of paper and do a rubbing with a soft-tipped pencil. Take away the leaf and then use the pencil to darken the outlined leaf drawing and its features. (You might be able to fit 3 to 4 leaves on each 8.5" × 11" sheet of paper.)
4. Using a tree guide, identify your tree types and write their common and Latin names under each leaf. Punch holes in each sheet to fit your binder and collect them inside.
5. When you discover new trees, add them to your collection, too!

## WORDS to KNOW

**BOTANIST:** A botanist is someone who studies plants.

# Plants That Save Lives

One of the sad effects of cutting down the rainforests is that scientists believe many of the plants found in them hold the key to curing human diseases. As a matter of fact, almost half of the drugs made in the United States came from the work done on wild plants. Some plant cures are simply amazing!

Before scientists discovered the medicine that could be made from the rosy periwinkle, 90 percent of all children that got childhood leukemia died from it. Then in the 1960s scientists began testing the small, pink flower from Madagascar. They discovered that extracts from the plant had a great healing effect. Now children have a 90 percent recovery rate from leukemia instead of 10 percent. All from a little pink flower from the rainforests of Madagascar! To the children suffering from that terrible disease, the rosy periwinkle is a miracle drug.

Other examples are just as stunning. As early as the 1700s, a doctor and botanist named William Wuthering discovered that when he ground up leaves of the wild-flower foxglove and gave it to a patient, it would cause their heart to beat harder. When he gave it to people in the middle of heart failure, the drug made their heart beat strongly again! This became a heart drug that is still used today, called digitalis.

## Visiting the Rainforest for Cures

Scientists make trips into the rainforest to talk to native peoples who use local plants to cure diseases. Considered folklore by many people for a long time, scientists finally began to realize that there must be a reason why natives have used these plants to cure illnesses for generations. The answer is, they work! The study of how natives use herbal treatments is called ethnobotany and has led to many great medical discoveries. There is a race against time now to discover what medicinal treasures are still to be found in our rainforests before they disappear forever under the clearing bulldozers' blades.

# Super Separates!

See how fast you can get each item through the maze and into the proper recycling bin. The only rule? Paths may cross each other, but may not travel together. Here's the fun part — there is more than one way to do this puzzle!

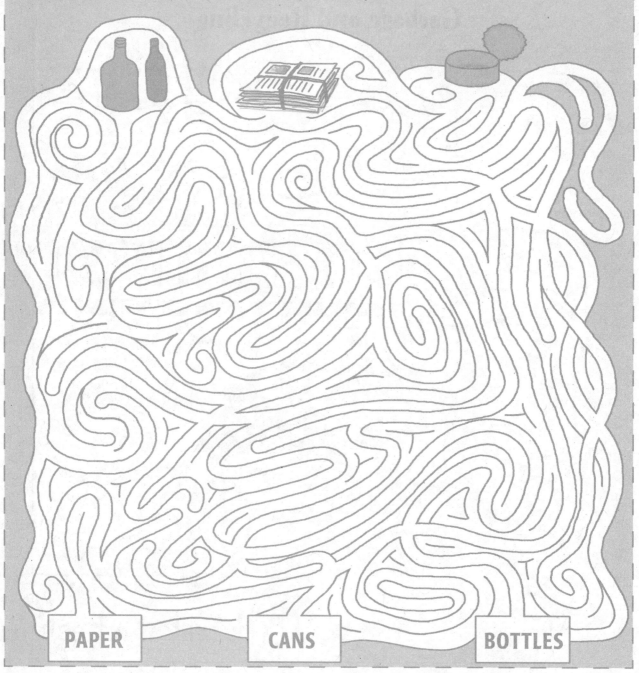

PAPER          CANS          BOTTLES

The EVERYTHING KIDS Environment Book

## Conservation Information

The best way to save our planet's resources is to use less of them! There are many things you can do in your everyday life to save or "conserve." You can also tell other people about the facts you collect about conservation. Once you have a list of things people can do, you can share that list with your parents, class, and neighbors. You can make up a few cool posters (on recycled paper, of course) and share them at school and in your neighborhood. Start a list of ways to conserve. By the end of this book you will have enough information to make a great informational poster and easy "green guidelines" to live by. Start with simple things like:

- Make recycling boxes for paper, magazines, newspaper, cardboard, cans, and bottles. Then be sure and use them!
- Recycle bottles and cans. Help out your parents by returning bottles and cans that have deposits. If you don't have time, bag them all up and bring them to the local Boy Scout or school bottle drive bins.
- Help your parents recycle shopping bags at your local grocery store.

Keep adding to your list over time. Recycling and saving gets addictive!

## Recycling

Americans use a lot of stuff in our everyday lives. If everyone recycled we would make a lot less garbage and use a lot less resources. Recycling works in a loop, but it only works if all

# Garbage into Gold

To do their job, the tiny organisms that turn plant waste into valuable compost need a blend of fresh green plants, dead brown plants, air, and water. Can you pick the six puzzle pieces that fit together to make the compost bin below? Careful — some of the pieces are turned!

The EVERYTHING KIDS' Environment Book

parts of the loop are going. The first part of the loop is when people, like you, recycle paper, bottles, cans, and plastics. The next part is when the recycled things get collected, cleaned, and sold to factories that can use them. Then the recyclables are made into new products like newspapers, carpets, and plastic tubs. Then people, like you, buy them again! That is the recycling loop. Whenever you buy a recycled product you are helping close the recycling loop. By recycling just 4 feet of paper, you could save one tree. If everyone in the United States recycled their newspaper just one day a week, we would save about 36 million trees a year. That's a whole forest! According to the Environmental Protection Agency (EPA), in 2005, Americans who recycled and composted stopped 64 million tons of stuff from going to landfills or being burned. That's 174 billion pounds of trash in one year alone! Recycling has an effect, and every little bit of recycling helps.

## When Did "Thinking Green" Start?

Americans recycled and conserved when we entered WWII (World War 2) in Europe, which lasted from 1939–1945. This was because some products, like meat, coffee, sugar, and tires became in short supply. But after the war, people became richer and they stopped worrying about resources as much. It was more than twenty years before people began to think "green" again. In the 1960s, the "environmental movement" started making people aware of how we were hurting the environment. People became more aware about littering, saving energy, growing organic foods, and recycling. But it would be another twenty years before it got expensive to take garbage to the landfills. That was what really got many people recycling. Today a lot of Americans do recycle. The EPA calculates that Americans recycle about ⅓ of their waste. Though recycling has increased, it is not something people have to do, so there is a lot more that people can do to conserve and reuse our valuable recourses.

# What Can Be Done ?

## Help with Recycling

Different states and towns have different recycling programs. Here are some tips to find out how to recycle where you live.

- Call your local recycling, solid waste, or public works department to find out what recycling programs are in your town.
- Ask your trash collector or at the local landfill about recycling in your area. Your state's environmental agency can help. To find out who and where they are check this Web site: *www.epa.gov/msw/states.htm*.
- If you are trying to recycle something big, like a washing machine, call the store where you bought it for information about how to recycle it.
- If you want to recycle electronic equipment, like computers, you can go to this Web site: *www.nrc-recycle.org/resources/electronics/index.htm*.

## Environmental Experiment

### The Compost Test

**Make some compost this winter in a small tub or pile in your yard. Follow the instructions on page 71 for a successful compost mix. You know your compost is ready when it is dark and earthy, like the inside of a chocolate cake.**

**In the spring dig a little garden spot in your yard, or use an existing garden spot or two big clay pots on your porch. You will need two spots of about the same size. They can be small for this test, just 1–2 square feet. You'll need a garden shovel and some flower seeds (or two small flowering plants of about the same size from your local nursery).**

1. Use your garden shovel and loosen up the soil in your two garden spots. If you are using two pots, fill both of them with soil right from your yard.
2. In one spot (or one pot) mix in some of the dark compost. Mix it up well with your shovel.
3. Now plant seeds (or a flowering plant) in each spot. Water them well.
4. Over the next few weeks, keep both spots equally watered and weeded.
5. After a few weeks do you notice a difference in how the seeds or plants are doing? Which one is doing better? Can you explain this difference?

## "Green" Tips

If you want to live a greener life, try not to buy or use too many things that can't be recycled. Try a different product that can be recycled. Here are some examples.

- Instead of buying paint in a spray can, which can't be recycled, buy a can of paint and a paintbrush. Make sure, when you are done with it, to throw away the paint can in a safe place. If you are not sure where, ask the people at your town landfill.
- Buy a lunch box and use it all year, instead of bringing lunches every day in paper or plastic bags.
- Ask your parents to try and only buy products that come in plastics with the #1 or #2 marked on the bottom. These are recyclables. Try not to buy products sold in plastic bottles marked with a #3, #4, #5, #6, and especially #7. You can help by going along on the next shopping trip and helping your parents look at the recycling numbers.
- Buy milk and juice in #2 plastic jugs and recycle them. Waxed cartons can't be recycled.
- Bring your own canvas bags to the grocery store to pack your food in.
- Try not to buy products with a lot of extra packaging, like plastic trays inside boxes with extra plastic wrapping. All that packaging uses resources and just has to be thrown away or recycled in the end anyway!
- Join and shop at your local food co-op. You can buy food in bulk with little or no packaging at all.

### How to Recycle Odd Things

You might be confused about how to recycle certain things. Learn what they are and how to do it. Make a list and post it at your school. This will help others know that there are places for recycling a lot of things that might have ended up at the landfill. Write a letter to the editor of your local paper telling everyone what they can recycle and how. Here are a few examples.

- People use a lot of ink cartridges in their computer printers. You can now recycle them through your local post office. Clear, plastic, stamped envelopes are available that you can package and send each cartridge in after it is empty. It won't cost you a penny!
- Old cell phones can be donated to people who need them. For how to do it, look on: *www.wirelessrecycling.com*
- Even your old computers can be recycled. Donate your old computers that still work to your local school or daycare center. If they don't work, you can recycle them through electronics recycling companies who will even pick them up at your home. Look online for "computer recycling."

## Composting Really Rots

Compost is actually rotting organic matter, like grass clippings, leaves, vegetable scraps, and bits of wood and straw. After decomposing it can be used to fertilize your garden. When mixed with some soil, the bacteria, fungi, worms, and insects will break down all the rotting matter, releasing the nutrients. This makes a rich fertilizer material that when added to the garden will help plants grow.

Composting is something that anyone can do. Besides making great fertilizer, it is a good way to get rid of garden waste without filling up our landfills. Here are some tips for easy composting.

- Use a plastic garbage can that can sit in your backyard. Or just make a pile in a corner of your yard.
- You can add vegetable kitchen scraps, egg shells,

## Try This

**Make Your Own Cool Art Paper Using Recycled Paper Grocery Bags**

**Making your own paper can be fun and the results really cool. To start you'll need a large square pan, about three inches deep (like a lasagna pan), a used paper grocery bag (reused until it starts to tear), a square of fine mesh window screen that will fit into the pan, a rolling pin, newspaper to work on, a blender, and an adult to run the blender.**

1. Tear the bag into tiny pieces.
2. Put the pieces and 3 cups of warm water into the blender, cover it, and turn it on medium speed for about five seconds until the paper is pulp.
3. Put the screen in the bottom of the pan and cover it with 1 inch of water.
4. Pour about a cup of the pulp over the screen and spread it around with your fingers.
5. Lift the screen carefully out of the pan and let the water drain away.
6. Then set it on an open section of newspaper. Close the newspaper over the top of the pulp. Flip it over so that the pulp is now face-down.
7. Use the rolling pin to roll out the extra water. Open the newspaper and carefully peel off the screen.
8. Let the pulp dry overnight. In the morning, peel your new sheet of paper off the newspaper. You have just recycled paper. Now paint something cool on it.

**Garbage and the Plague**

In the years 1347–1351 the bubonic plague, also called the "black death," spread through Europe, Asia, and Africa, killing 75 million people. What they didn't know at the time was that it was all caused by too much garbage in the streets! Piles of garbage attracted rats, which had fleas, which carried the disease. The rats carried the plague from place to place. The lack of sanitation made the spread of the plague the worst in human history.

and coffee grounds. Don't add any meat scraps. A mixture of different kinds of things, like grass, leaves, and food scraps are the best.

- Add some plain dirt to the mixture now and then, if you have some available.
- Decomposing compost needs air, so the pile (or the garbage can) will have to be stirred with a shovel every time you add more materials. It will get hot when it is decomposing. If it doesn't rain you may have to water your compost a little to keep it moist (but not too wet—or it will mold).
- When the rich, dark, earthy material is all ready, add it to your garden. Your plants will love it!

# What's in a Shopping Bag?

If you have gone food shopping then you have probably heard the checkout person ask, "Paper or plastic?" The best answer, of course, is neither. If you can, you should bring your own tote bags to the food store to save on using so many shopping bags every week. If you have to choose though, which shopping bag is worse for the environment? Paper bags are made from natural fibers that come from lumber waste. Plastic bags are made from the waste that is left over when oil is cleaned. Paper bags, if left out in the sun and rain, will break down or "biodegrade." Plastic bags will last for a very long time even if left out in sun and rain.

Even knowing all this, plastic shopping bags are still thought to be better for the environment to use than paper shopping bags. How can this be? We'll compare them. Research has shown that making paper bags from trees grown on plantations takes more energy than plastic bags made from oil refinery waste. Paper bags take up about seven times the space of plastic bags and take more energy and cost to ship to stores. Paper bags take up much more room in the landfills than plastic. Paper may break down faster than plastic, but only if it is exposed to the elements. In a packed and covered landfill, they will last a long time too. Overall, it is best to bring your own shopping bags to the grocery store if you can. Store them under the seat in your car, so you have them the next time you shop. If you do take paper or plastic shopping bags from the store, save them and use them until they fall apart. Paper grocery bags are great for covering schoolbooks. See if your food store will put in a recyclable plastic bag collection bin.

### How Plastic Bags Can Be Dangerous

Plastic bags that are lost in the wind travel a long way. Sometimes they can blow out into the ocean. Here they can hurt ocean animals. As you read in the ocean pollution chapter, sea turtles sometimes eat plastic bags, thinking they are jellyfish. This can block their stomach and make them starve. Seals, whales, and dolphins can also be hurt the same way. Plastic bags also get pushed in the wind against fences, building up into an ugly mess. They clog drains, sewers, and intake fans. They have caused such a problem in some countries that they have been banned, and people who still use them are taxed or fined.

## Our Leaking Landfills

When people started farming about 10,000 years ago, they mostly gave up their wandering, hunting, gathering lives and settled down. With all those people living in one place for a long time, they started to build up a lot of garbage. This was how the first garbage dumps were born. People have been making garbage dumps for as long as they have been living in one place. Even Native Americans from thousands of years ago, after a big buffalo hunt, would leave behind a pile of garbage that was as big as dumps today. As early as 500 B.C. it's believed that the Greeks created dumps outside of their cities. Amazingly, many of those ancient dumps are now important archeological sites! You can learn a lot about a people from what is in their garbage dumps.

## What Can Be Done

### What Can Be Done to Make Less Trash?

There are many ways people can make less trash. This helps cut down on the amount of trash going into our landfills, but it also helps us use fewer new resources, like trees, water, and oil. You might think that what you do is so small that it won't make a difference. But every little bit helps. To make less trash you can:

1. Recycle and buy recycled products.
2. Send e-cards instead of using paper cards.
3. Use cloth napkins instead of paper napkins.
4. Use Tupperware instead of plastic bags.
5. Look for products that have less packaging.
6. Use rechargeable batteries.
7. Use a lunch box instead of paper or plastic sacks.
8. Buy a water bottle and carry it with you, so you can stop buying bottled water.
9. Give water bottles as gifts, so everyone can stop buying bottled water!

## Early Trash

The first European settlers in America dealt with their garbage by dumping it over their back fence, in the river, or burying it in their yards. They often burned garbage too. Then as communities grew into towns, they made town dumps. Now we call garbage dumps landfills. Sadly, many early landfills were made in wetlands, which were thought to be wasteland back then. Early landfills leaked into rivers and lakes. They used to catch fire and even explode sometimes, because as garbage rots, it gives off methane, a flammable gas. The first garbage-burning plant, called an incinerator, in the United States was built on Governor's Island in New York in 1885. By 1914, there were 300 incinerators burning garbage in the United States.

## Garbage Today

Landfills have changed a lot from the first city dump. As of 1995, there were more than 2,500 landfills in the United States. In 1993, a law was passed that all landfills must be lined with a big plastic liner to keep them from leaking into the environment. They also have to have "gas monitors" to keep track of the dangerous gases that build up. Researchers have found that Americans each make about 4.5 pounds of garage every day. The United States makes more garbage than any other country on the planet. We have 5 percent of the people on Earth, but make almost one-third of all the world's garbage! So as landfills keep filling up, people will have to find more places for all that trash. Landfills will be buried,

The EVERYTHING KIDS' Environment Book

DINOS $1.10 each

JIGSAW JIGSAW JIGSAW

PUZZLES 50¢ each

75¢

15¢

BLOCKS $2.00

CARS 5¢ each

SKATES $3.00

BOOKS 10¢ each

$1.50

25¢

# Junk into Cash

Evan has cleaned out his room. Instead of throwing his old stuff in the trash, he decided to have a tag sale! What six items does Evan need to sell to make four dollars?

*Extra Fun:* Evan wants to buy a bird feeder for his family. If he sells all the stuff at his tag sale, which bird feeder can he afford to buy?

$13.20

$15.75

$8.10

# 500 Billion Bags!

**That's how many plastic bags are given out at grocery stores each year. How many of those are recycled? Less than three percent! Break the code below to learn how you can help reduce this huge amount of waste.**

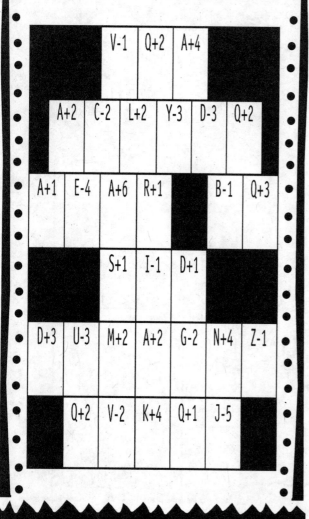

| | V-1 | Q+2 | A+4 | | |
|---|---|---|---|---|---|
| A+2 | C-2 | L+2 | Y-3 | D-3 | Q+2 |
| A+1 | E-4 | A+6 | R+1 | | B-1 | Q+3 |
| | S+1 | I-1 | D+1 | | |
| D+3 | U-3 | M+2 | A+2 | G-2 | N+4 | Z-1 |
| | Q+2 | V-2 | K+4 | Q+1 | J-5 | |

landscaped, and reclaimed into golf courses or city parks all over America.

## The Garbage Barge That No One Wanted

In 1987, a barge carrying more than 6 million pounds of garbage left Islip, New York, to head down the coast to a methane-producing landfill in North Carolina. When they got there the garbage was turned away because it had hospital trash, considered toxic waste, in the batch. After two weeks, with no place to go, they went on to Louisiana, where they were once again rejected. The next stop was Mexico, where the Mexican Navy blocked them from even entering their waters. Then Belize and the Bahamas sent them away. Finally, they headed back north and sat in the harbor off Long Island until October while people battled in court about who would get stuck with all that garbage! Finally, it was settled. The garbage was burned in an incinerator in Brooklyn and the 840,000 pounds of ash went back to Islip to the very landfill that had rejected all that garbage back in the first place.

# WORDS to KNOW

**TOXIC WASTE**: Toxic waste is trash that can harm or kill living things, including people. It is often chemicals, but can be medical waste.

# Chapter 7
# Environmentalism and Green Living

# Powered by the Sun

Solar power is energy produced by the sun in the form of heat and light. Even though the sun is 93 million miles away from Earth, it takes only about 8 minutes for this energy to reach us! If people used more solar energy, we could conserve other fuels like coal, oil, and natural gas.

The following words are nothing without the power of the letters S-U-N. See if you can finish each word using the clues provided.

S U N _ _ _ = ice cream with sauce and whipped cream

S U N _ = fell to the bottom of the sea

S U N _ _ _ _ = window in the top of a car

_ S U N _ _ _ = dangerous ocean wave

S U _ _ _ N = very quickly

S _ U _ N _ = press your eyes into tiny slits

_ _ S _ _ U N _ = cut the price

S _ U N _ = stabbed by a bee

_ _ S _ _ U N _ = put new strings on a guitar

S _ _ U N _ = made much smaller

# The High Cost of Energy

If you knew how much energy it took to make things, would you try to use less stuff? You might be surprised to learn the high cost in energy of the things you use every day. These estimates might make you go green, and that's a good thing! Here are some things you should know.

- A regular toilet uses 8 gallons of water every time you flush. It's estimated that every day Americans use 4.8 billion gallons of clean water just to flush their toilets. That's almost half the water we use indoors every day!
- If every home in America bought just one roll of 100 percent recycled paper towels, it would save more than a half million trees.
- Every year we throw away 20 million tons of electronics, like old computers, radios, and CD players.
- Recycling an aluminum can takes just 5 percent of the energy it takes to mine and refine that amount of new aluminum.

Do you feel like getting greener yet?

## Energy from the Sun

Solar energy is a "renewable resource." This means that you can use it, and more is being made all the time. As long as the sun is shining, more energy will be there for us to use. Solar energy is collected for heating homes, businesses, and water. It's used to dry out agricultural grains like wheat and corn, herbs, and fruit. People use solar power to heat pools, greenhouses, and arboretums. Solar power charges emergency phones on American highways, keeps streetlights lit, and powers flashing road signs. Builders have even developed solar roof shingles!

## TryThis

**Feel the Burn!**

Stand in front of a window directly in the sun (this works in winter or summer). You can feel the heat from the sun on your skin, even though you are behind glass. If you keep standing there, you will feel hotter and hotter. Stay as long as you can until you start to feel sweat break out on your skin. Now step away from the window into the shade. Can you feel the temperature difference? This is passive solar energy and it really works to heat sunny rooms.

## WORDS to KNOW

**SEMICONDUCTOR:** A semiconductor is a material that can carry the electrical charge made by the sunlight. Most solar semiconductors are a layer of silicon.

**WATT:** A watt is a unit of power and how we measure electricity. A regular light bulb usually uses between 40 and 100 watts of electricity. The 100-watt bulb is brighter and uses more units of power.

## The Sun Lighting Our Homes

Solar power can even be made into electricity. This is called "photovoltaics." Photovoltaic energy is when sunlight is collected by a "solar cell" and then passed through a special "semiconductor" to create an electrical flow. This was actually discovered accidentally by researchers at the telephone company in 1954, who were looking at how silicon reacted to sunlight.

Many solar cells are connected together into larger arrays to collect more power. The more solar cells there are, the more "watts" of energy they collect. Solar cells are not mechanical, so they take no energy to run and no water or cooling to convert sunlight to electricity. They make no waste that has to be thrown away. This is a clean and renewable energy.

## The Dark Side of Solar Power

The only problem with solar power is that it's not always sunny outside! Some places have more cloud cover that blocks sunlight, and of course there is no solar power collection at night. The ideal place for solar power is an area where there is little cloud cover, like a desert or other arid region that has some room for solar collectors to lie out and take in the sunshine. In the United States, the southwestern part of the country has the sunniest climate for solar collection, but homes everywhere can benefit from some solar collection. Even just big, south-facing windows can bring solar heat into a home. This is called passive solar collection.

## The Space for Solar

The other problem with solar power is that you need a big area facing the sun to collect it. On a single home, the collection area can be on a rooftop facing the sun, but what about a tall building with many apartments? Or a whole city? It takes space to collect solar power. It is hard for big power companies to collect and sell solar power because sunlight collection takes a lot of space. There were only fourteen known large, solar-electric generating units working in the United States in 2004, all of them in California and Arizona.

Solar science has also only worked out how to make about 25 percent of the sunlight we get into power. Plus the silicon and metals in solar cells are very stiff and hard, so they can't be used for a lot of things that aren't flat. New plastic semiconductors are much more flexible and easier to make, but they only make 10 percent of the sunlight into power. Solar science

The EVERYTHING KIDS' Environment Book

# TryThis

## Have a Windmill Party

**At your next party, make windmills! All you need are squares of paper 8.5" × 8.5" (Hint: You can use regular copy paper and cut 2.5 inches off the end to make it square. This is a great way to use up junk mail paper that hasn't been folded.) You will need enough squares of paper, thumbtacks, and pencils for each person making a windmill. You will also need some scissors and an adult helper to use them.**

1. After your grownup helper has cut your squares, have everyone color their squares on both sides, with markers or crayons.

2. Ask your grownup helper to cut each square four times, one cut from each corner to about one inch from the center.

3. Have everyone take their thumbtack and push it into the pencil just below where the metal eraser band ends. Now pull it out again. That hole is where you will attach your windmill.

4. To fold your windmill, hold your newly cut square in your left hand between your thumb and forefinger. Try to keep your thumb right in the middle of the square (you'll have to push your hand down into one of the cuts to reach the center with your thumb).

5. With your right hand take the right corner of each cut section and fold it over in an arch to the center, trapping the tip under your thumb. (Don't crease the paper.)

6. Do this for all four sections. You have to keep all four tips under your thumb. This is a little tricky, especially if you all start giggling!

7. Now take your thumbtack and push it through all four tips and the center of your paper and pin it back into your pencil. You may need some help from your grownup helper.

8. You have made a windmill. Take it outside into the wind and watch it spin!

still has a long way to go to be the endless, clean, free power we hope it will be, but it's getting there!

## Harnessing the Wind

The wind is renewable energy because it never stops blowing! It flows around the planet pushed on by the uneven heating and cooling of the earth's surface. It is an endless supply of power, if only we can harness it.

As soon as humans took to the ocean in boats they began using wind power for sailing. Then farmers fastened early wind turbines into windmills. They used them to grind grain and pull up water from wells. Even early lumber mills were powered by windmills. In the early 1900s, when electricity had not made it out to rural ranches in the American west, ranchers put up small windmills to generate their own electricity.

Nowadays wind energy is mostly used for making electricity. The turning blades power a generator

# On the Right Track

**United Parcel Service saved a huge amount of energy by changing how they deliver packages in big cities. To find out what they did, put each letter in its proper place in the grid. The letters all fit in spaces under their own column, but maybe not in the same order! We left some letters to get you started.**

| M | R | I |   | A |   | L |   | S |   |   | T |   |   |
| D | A | O | Y | S | T | T | R | I | N |   | I | T | O |
| G | A | S | D | E | D | N | R | N | T | F | I | G | O |
| C | H | N | E | W | R | I | N | T | R | R | W | O | S | T | E |
|   | R | V |   |   | S |   |   |   | Y |   |   |   |   |
|   | K |   |   | O |   |   | Y |   |   |   |   | H | T |
| H |   |   |   | U |   |   |   |   |   | S |   |   |   |
| T |   | E |   | O |   | ' |   |   |   | A |   |   |   |
|   | A |   |   |   | T |   |   | G |   |   |   |   |   |
|   |   | S |   |   |   | A | F |   |   | C | ! |   |   |

The EVERYTHING KID Environment Book

that turns the mechanical power into electricity. Modern windmills are called wind machines, and they are huge. One wind machine can be as tall as a twenty-story building with three blades that are 200 feet long. They are placed in wide-open areas, often near the coasts where the wind blows a lot of the time.

More and more states are starting to make wind farms to help supply people with the electricity they need. The state of California makes more than twice as much wind power as any other of the thirty states using it. But they only work when the wind is blowing!

### Ocean Breeze

Because of the wind stirred up off the ocean, many wind farms are being planned for offshore sites. The first offshore wind farm in the United States is planned for off the coast of Cape Cod, Massachusetts. According to wind power experts, each windmill will be able to make up to 4 million kilowatt hours (kWh) of electricity per year. That will supply up to 400 homes.

Wind farms with dozens of wind machines can make electricity for entire communities. A wind farm in Texas has 46 wind machines that make enough electricity for 7,300 homes. Wind farms are usually owned by people or businesses, which then sell the power to public power companies. In the United States today, wind machines are making enough electricity to supply about 1.6 million homes. That may sound like a lot but in a country as big as ours, it is still less than 1 percent of the people. It is growing over time though. In just the last ten years, the amount of wind power has grown 300 percent.

# Water Power

Power from water can be made in many different ways. The most common way is through a hydroelectric dam. This is where a river is blocked until the water builds up into a large lake, or reservoir, behind a tall dam wall.

## Did You Know?

### A Fish with a Ladder

To protect salmon and other spawning fish that are blocked by dams, fish ladders were created. A fish ladder (also called a fish way or fish pass) is a man-made structure built around a dam to allow fish to still make their way upstream to spawn. They are often a chain of low steps up, which the fish can leap. The flow of water has to be just right to attract the fish to the ladder but not tire it out.

## Environmental Experiment

### Organic Taste Test

Do foods grown organically taste better than foods grown with chemicals? You can do a test to find out. You will need to go to your local food co-op and buy a few things. Try a few organic foods like an apple, cheddar cheese, and carrots. Now buy the same foods from your grocery store. Make sure they are not organic (most stores have special displays for their organic foods). You will need some taste-testing volunteers and a grownup to help you cut up the food. Have a paper and pencil to write down the comments from each taste tester about the foods they tried.

1. Have them each taste a slice of apple. Do not tell them if it is organic or not!
2. Give them each a sip of water. Then have them each taste a slice of the other kind of apple.
3. Ask them which tasted better and why. Write down their responses.
4. Try this with all the foods you bought.
5. Afterward, see how the comments rated the organic food compared to the chemically treated food. What did you find out?

The water is released through an opening over the dam and as it falls, it flows through a machine called a turbine and turns the propellers attached to an electric generator. This creates the electricity. The greater height from which the water falls, the more power it makes.

Natural waterfalls like Niagara Falls work in much the same way. The power in the falling water makes the generator work, which makes the electricity. It is gravity working on the water that gives us this power. Power lines connected to the generator carry the electricity where it needs to go.

Hydroelectric power is a clean and renewable power source. There is no pollution given off while using hydroelectric power. The reservoir behind the dam can be a place for people to swim, boat, and fish. Farmers can use some of the water for irrigation of their fields. A dam, once built, can last for 100 years.

### The Dark Side of Dams

There are a few bad things about dams that are important to know. To build a hydroelectric dam, a large area must be flooded behind the dam to make the reservoir. Whole communities sometimes have to be moved to another place. Entire forests can be drowned. Rotting vegetation under the water can give off methane. The water released from the dam can be colder than usual and this can affect the ecosystems in the rivers downstream. It can also cause erosion downstream, washing away riverbanks and scraping away life on the river bottom. The worst effect of dams has been seen on salmon that have to travel upstream to spawn, or lay their eggs. If blocked by a dam, the salmon life cycle (and that of many other fish) cannot be completed. To try and solve this, fish experts designed fish ladders to get fish over the dam.

### Tidal Power

Other forms of water power include capturing the energy of the rising and falling tides. In some ways, tide power is more dependable than wind and solar power because the tides go in and out all day and night at a rate we know. Though tides never change, they do grow during storms and, because they are controlled by the gravitational pull of the moon, the tides do differ according to what phase the moon is in. People have been using the tides to power little coastal mills to grind grain for generations.

## River Power

Another form of water power is a simple water wheel placed in a river. The water flowing down-stream turns the wheel and generates power. The water wheel has been used to mill grains, mine ore, pump water, and power iron forges for more than a thousand years.

# Organic Farming— No More Yucky Chemicals

Organic foods are fruits, vegetables, grains, and dairy products that are grown without using chemicals, like man-made pesticides and fertilizers. The food also cannot have chemicals added to it later or be exposed to radiation (food manufacturers sometimes do this to oils and other foods to keep them from going bad while they wait on store shelves to be sold). To be considered organic, plants themselves also can't be genetically altered. Organic meat comes from animals that have had no hormones or antibiotics.

People like organic foods because they consider them more pure, healthy, and tasty. With no additives there is no chance that you will be eating chemicals that you don't want in your body. The National Research Council (NRC) has found through a study that children and babies take in the pesticides from the foods they eat and the pesticides build up in their bodies. A study by the U.S. Department of Agriculture found that pesticides stayed on fruits and vegetables even after they'd been washed and even peeled! To protect their kids and

# Dump Not!

Find words from the list in the dump. Use a colored marker to highlight these items. They don't need to be dumped — they can be recycled and reused! Hint: Words can be up, down, backwards, or diagonal.

STEEL    PLASTIC    MAGAZINES
PAPER    SODA CANS    ALUMINUM
CLOTH    MILK JUGS    MOTOR OIL
GLASS    CARDBOARD    CAR BATTERIES

```
        A B C U D
      U E D F G B H
      I U S T E E L
    J B K L M N O B P D L
U M A G A Z I N E S I Q
R D S D T V U W X O Y U
B Z P A P E R A R B B C
U D E L B F G O H I J S
S K B U L M T N B O E P
O Q R M D O S D T I U U
D U V I M W B X R P Y B
A Z A N B U C E D L E F
C G B U D H T I J A K M
A L M M N T O P Q S R I
N S U T A U D U V T U L
S W X B Y U Z A B I D K
C D R A O B D R A C D J
E A F G H I J B D K D U
C D L U M C L O T H N G
S S A L G X U Y U Z A S
```

## Organic Is Green

Many people think that growing foods organically is better for the environment. Farms that grow organic foods have no chemicals running off their land into lakes and streams. Birds that land in organic farm fields are not exposed to chemical pesticides. Butterflies and honeybees can live on or near organic farms without being killed accidentally by pesticides meant for farm pests. Even the people who work on organic farms have a healthier environment. Exposure to pesticides can make workers feel sick and over a long period of time can make someone very ill. According to the World Health Organization, three million people are poisoned every year by pesticides and 220,000 of them die. About 10 percent of the 70,000 chemicals used in the United States can cause cancer. Chemical pesticides should at least make people wonder.

## Why Do They Use Chemicals?

The reason pesticides and fertilizers are used is that people think they make food easier to grow. Farmers lose less food to pests and they can add nutrients to the ground that are lost from growing crop after crop, year after year. Organic foods are more expensive to buy, partly because there are less of them available. As people ask for more and more organic foods, more will be raised and sold and hopefully over time we will find organic foods everywhere.

## Frankenfoods

Everything about us from the color of our eyes and hair to our height is mapped out in our genes. It is the same in plants. The fruits and vegetables that we grow have genes too. That is what makes an apple red or green, sweet or sour, crispy or soft. Those genes can be changed if we want a special kind of trait, like sweeter taste. Farmers have been doing this for hundreds of years. Instead of letting their plants be pollinated by the bees in any way that happens, the farmer takes the pollen from a plant with sweeter fruit and uses it to pollinate the plant with better color. After a while they get the fruit they want and they use that plant over and over. A new kind of apple has been made! This is a form of genetic engineering.

Food scientists have taken this a step further by adding genes to plants in the laboratory to give them the traits they want. They can add genes that keep plants from growing moldy in the field or allow them to survive dry weather or even kill the insect pests that eat them. Scientists have also added vitamins to plants, like rice, so when people grow them they get more vitamins right in their food.

The good side of GM (genetically modified) food is that there is more food being grown, with less waste and

## WORDS to KNOW

**GENES:** Genes are the smallest unit of heredity. We have more than 20,000 genes that map out all of our traits from eye color to earlobe shape.

**GENETICALLY MODIFIED (GM) FOOD:** Genetically modified (GM) food is grown from plants that have had some of their genes altered by scientists to give them traits that they want.

much less pesticides used. For poor countries, where some people can only afford rice to eat, the vitamin rice is helpful.

The bad side of GM food is that people are afraid of what the genetic engineering of plants may do in the long run. They have nicknamed them "Frankenfoods" after the Frankenstein monster in the fictional story who was put together from spare parts! Will it make it harder for small farms here and in poorer countries to afford seeds? Will it change plants forever in ways that they would not have naturally done? Will it affect the people who eat them in some way we don't see yet? All these questions have made some countries ban GM foods or put strong limits on them. Some people won't eat

them at all. Only time will tell if GM foods are completely safe or will be accepted by people as the next stage in food production.

## Heroic Environmentalists

Throughout history certain people have made it their mission to speak out against the wrongs others were doing to the environment and take a stand to protect our fragile Earth. Here are some of the most well-known heroic environmentalists.

### The Foremother–Rachel Carson

Rachel Carson has been called "the mother of the modern environmental movement." She

was an outdoorswoman who spent a lot of time exploring the forests of Pennsylvania and the rocky coast of Maine. She loved nature and the things she wrote about the environment have stirred people throughout time to value and protect the earth.

A biologist for the U.S. Fish and Wildlife Service, Rachel Carson believed that though humans are part of nature, they also have the power to hurt the natural environment. She worried about people using chemical pesticides and she wrote about it in her famous book called *Silent Spring*. The book warned people about the dangers of using pesticides and how it could affect the environment and human health. She testified in front of Congress in 1963, calling for new policies to protect the environment and people from the use of chemicals. This action and her book, made such an impression on President Kennedy (and others) that he ordered the testing of the chemicals of which she wrote.

Sadly, Rachel Carson developed breast cancer and died in 1964, but her life and books have encouraged a whole generation to protect the environment.

## The Spirit of the Trees—John Muir

Sometimes a great environmentalist does their job just by telling stories. That was John Muir's gift. Through the stories he wrote about his life in the Sierra Nevada Mountains of California, he affected millions of people. One of our earliest conservationists, he lived from 1838–1914. He started the Sierra Club, an important conservation organization, and helped to save the Yosemite Valley and other wilderness areas. He believed that we needed

### Did You Know?

**The Butterfly and the Redwood**

In 1997 a young woman named Julia Butterfly Hill climbed into a giant redwood that was going to be cut down and refused to come down. She stayed in the tree (named Luna) for two years! She finally came down when an agreement could be reached with the lumber company not to cut the tree down.

to save wilderness not for its money value or even its biodiversity, but for its own sake and for its spiritual effect on mankind. He helped to change the way we look at the natural world.

## Treating Our Closest Relatives Better—Jane Goodall

Jane Goodall lived in the jungles of Africa for twenty-five years and watched chimpanzees live their lives. The things she saw taught us a lot about our closest animal relatives. It changed how people thought about chimpanzees and made us think about how we treat primates throughout the world. In 1977 she founded the Jane Goodall Institute to help save habitats, teach about the environment, and keep primate research and protection going in Africa. To this day, Jane Goodall spends much of her time speaking around the world and sharing her message of hope for the future. She wants to encourage young people to make a difference in their world.

# The Environmental Protection Agency

In 1970 the United States government formed the Environmental Protection Agency (EPA). The EPA was formed because people were demanding cleaner water, air, and land. Before that time, the government had no way to deal with the pollutants that were hurting people and the environment. The EPA had to try and fix all the damage that had been done to the environment and make new guidelines for Americans to keep it that way. Our Congress makes the laws about the environment and the EPA makes sure people and businesses follow them.

## Taking Action Against Polluters

If people or businesses don't meet pollution standards, the EPA can take action against them. The EPA can help pay for environmental programs to study problems, clean them up, and educate the public so they can help, too. In 1982 the EPA set aside a lot of money to clean up places in the United States that had been damaged by the dumping of dangerous pollutants. These were called superfund sites, because of the high cost of cleaning up the dangerous toxic pollutants. The EPA works with industries, businesses, and state and local governments to:

- Stop pollution by lowering greenhouse gases, indoor air pollution, and toxic waste releases.
- Reuse solid waste whenever they can.
- Get control of pesticide risks.
- Save water and energy.

In return, the EPA encourages everyone to follow the rules by letting the public (you and me) know when a company is doing good environmental work. One of the most important goals of the EPA is to teach everyone how to be aware of, care for, and feel responsible for the environment. It is only through people knowing how and doing their part to take care of the earth that we can keep our environment safe for generations to come.

# Chapter 8

# Ways You Can Help the Environment

# Thinking Green

The word *green* has become symbolic for environmental awareness. When you are "thinking green" it means you are looking for ways in your everyday life to help protect the environment. That can include ways to save energy, reduce trash, create less pollution, use less water and resources, drive less, give more to organizations that work to save endangered animals and habitats, and share what you know with others.

When people build "green homes" they build in ways to save resources over time. They often use materials that are recycled and are safer to live with. In Europe, the government is letting people pay fewer taxes if they make their homes more energy efficient. Following are some of the things people put in a green home. Share these ideas with your parents.

- Low-flow showers, toilets, and washers that use less water
- Big south-facing windows with insulated shades, to save on heat
- Good insulation made from recycled paper cellulose to keep heat inside in the winter and outside in the summer
- Solar panels for heating water and radiant heat floors
- Recycled plastic carpets, decks, and even roof tiles
- Landscaping with native plants that don't need extra water or any fertilizer

## How You Can Help Your Family Be Green

If you want to live green and save energy, there are many things you can do around the house and yard. Offer to rake the yard, walks, and driveway for your parents and neighbors so no one needs to use electrical equipment like leaf-blowers. Machines use a lot of energy and the wind will bring those leaves back anyway! If your yard is small, you can use a push mower instead of a gas mower. Raking and hand mowing is actually kind of fun and it is really good exercise, too.

Thinking green is about not polluting too. Try spraying soapy water on your houseplants or garden vegetables if they get pests on them. It can work as well as chemical pesticides and it is not poisonous. Ask your parents to buy biodegradable cleaning products so that cleaning your house doesn't hurt the soil and water system. Never, ever pour antifreeze, oil, or other chemicals on the ground, into storm sewers, or down the drain. Find out where your local waste disposal facility is and let your parents know. Also find out when the next toxic waste day is at your town landfill and talk to your parents about getting rid of old paint cans and other yucky stuff in your basement and garage. Throwing out toxic waste properly makes the world a safer place and your home should be the safest place on Earth!

## Your Energy-Wasting Lawn

According to the EPA, Americans have covered 25 million acres of our country with lawns. That is roughly about the size of the state of Pennsylvania. Lawns use tons of water, are often treated with chemical fertilizers and weed killers, and need to be cut every week or more. Lawn mowers, edgers, weed whackers, and hedge trimmers all are expensive and need gallons and gallons of gas to run. They are also noisy! Lawns replace natural habitats of native plants that are used by birds, butterflies, and other animals. Ask your parents if you could plant some native bushes. These bushes are good cover for birds and other animals, reduce the amount of grass to be mowed, and can be very pretty!

## Join an Environmental Group and Go Green!

There are many great environmental groups that you and your family can join. Ask for a membership for your birthday and give them to others as gifts. You can start by looking at their Web sites to see if what they do is something you want to help with. Some groups work to save all wildlife, while others focus on birds or a certain kind of animal. Some groups save all habitats, while others pay attention to just rainforests or deserts or grasslands or the ocean. Some groups work in Washington, D.C., on environmental laws. Here are a few of the most common environmental groups and their Web sites.

- **The Sierra Club** works to save our national parks and wilderness areas. *www.sierraclub.org*
- **The World Wildlife Fund** works to protect the world's wildlife and wildlands. *www.worldwildlife.org*
- **The Rainforest Alliance** works to save tropical rainforests all over the world. *www.rainforest-alliance.org*
- **The Nature Conservancy** works to save plants and animals by protecting their habitats. *www.nature.org*
- **The National Wildlife Federation** works to protect nature and wildlife. *www.nwf.org*
- **Greenpeace, USA** works to preserve the earth and the life it supports. *www.greenpeaceusa.org*

**Try This**

**Design Your Ideal Green House**

Just for fun design the perfect green house. Take a big sheet of paper and draw your ideal house. Add a windmill in the yard and solar panels on the roof. Make a garden with vegetables and plants that would live in your climate. You can make it really fun and have it be in a tree or built into the side of a hill. Show the inside rooms with big solar windows, plants, and a recycling pantry. Make your room really cool, too!

**Did You Know?**

**How Does Your Lawn Pollute the Air?**

Even small lawns use a lot of energy. Mowing a lawn that is only a ¼ acre makes more air pollution than driving a car from New York to Washington, D.C., and back.

## Start Your Own Green Group

When you and your friends first meet to start your own "green group" you have some decisions to make. What kinds of things do you want to do? Do you want to help save the environment or just teach other people how to think green? Do you want to focus on saving all wildlife or one kind of animal, like tigers, that you love? Once you decide on your mission you can come up with a group name and a mission statement. The mission statement tells what you hope to do in your green group.

You also have to decide how much time you and your group can commit to your goals. One hour a week? Two? Make it a reasonable amount of time so everyone can make it.

Everyone in the group should have something to do to help out. Think about what skills each of the members of your group have. Is there an artist who can make posters? Is there a computer expert who can make you a Web site? Who wants to take notes, make phone calls, and do research online? At whose house will you meet, or will you ask to use a room in school after hours? Maybe a meeting during lunch would be fun, too. You should consider having a grownup advisor to help out, too.

At the end of each meeting, plan what you will do at your next meeting so everyone has something to look forward to. Make sure everyone gets a chance to speak and be heard. That is what makes a group work well. Don't worry if someone misses a meeting, but maybe call her up later and tell her what she missed.

Decide if you want to invite anyone else to join the group or keep it just a friends group. If

# Jar Art

Some materials can be recycled without ever leaving the house! What could you do with these empty jars? Break the Vowel-Switch code to find out. Then use your markers or crayons to complete the transformation!

COTCH LAGHTNANG BIGS

VOSU FER WALD FLEWURS

STERU LUFTEVURS AN FRADGU

CELLUCT ELD BITTANS

you decide that you want more members, you will have to advertise with posters or announcements at school. It's a great way to make new friends.

Do you need to raise money to make fliers or give money to a cause that your group wants to help? Here are some ideas about how to raise money for your group.

- Return cans and bottles for the deposit.
- Organize a car wash in front of your school. Charge $5 per car and put all the money in your collection. Be sure and get permission from your principal first.
- Ask your parents to help you apply for grants from local organizations.
- Have a bake sale. Make it fun by making cookies shaped like animals, mountains, and trees!

Check out all the environmental groups at the end of this book and see what they each do. Maybe you can model your goals after one of them. Have fun!

## Planting Trees

Planting trees is a fun way to act green and help the environment. All trees, as you now know, make oxygen and take away carbon dioxide. They also hold the soil with their roots, add shade and shelter for wildlife, cool the air temperature, lower noise pollution, and block wind. They are worth adding to your neighborhood!

Trees are amazing living things. They have the longest lives of any organism on Earth. Each tree makes 260 pounds of oxygen a year. An acre of trees supplies enough oxygen in a year for eighteen people to breathe. One of the

# Four Fast Fixes

Choose words from the dark box that rhyme with each of the words in the sentences below. Write them on the lines provided. When you are finished, you will learn four things you can do to help save energy and resources! Hint: It helps to read each sentence aloud and slowly.

LOSE OATH STRIDES DOVE HAY CEASE DOVE VAPOR

_____

BURN COUGH BITES MEN VIEW WEAVE HAY TOMB

_____

FOOT PLANS TWIN DUH WEE-MICHAEL CHIN

_____

LEARN SCOFF DAUGHTER GLEN BLUSHING WREATH

_____

| | | | | |
|---|---|---|---|---|
| USE | OFF | SIDES | PAPER | OFF |
| LIGHTS | WHEN | YOU | TURN | IN |
| LEAVE | PUT | ROOM | CANS | OF |
| PIECE | BOTH | THE | BIN | A |
| WATER | BOTH | THE | BIN | OF |
| BRUSHING | WHEN | TEETH | RECYCLE | A |

The EVERYTHING KIDS' Environment Book

tallest trees known on Earth is a giant redwood sequoia in California. It is 275 ft. (84 m) tall. That's a lot of oxygen-making potential!

## The Man Who Planted Trees

You have probably heard the name Johnny Appleseed, but you might not have known that he was a real person. His name was John Chapman and he lived in Massachusetts in the late 1700s. He made a name for himself by exploring the frontier wilderness, mostly in bare feet, and planting apple trees wherever he went. He didn't just plant seeds either. He found a good spot in the wilderness, cleared the brush, planted seeds and built a fence to protect them from animals. Some of his orchards covered many acres. When settlers moved into the area to start farms, they were very happy to see apple orchards already grown and making fruit. Many orchards in western New York, Pennsylvania, Ohio, Michigan, Indiana, and Illinois are thought to have been started by John Chapman's seeds. Some think he planted millions of seeds in his years in the wilderness.

## Picking Trees to Plant

There are a few ways you can get trees to plant. You can ask your parents to call your county cooperative extension, soil and water conservation district, or just a local nursery. The best time to plant trees is in the spring when it is still cool. Then the tree has all summer to grow and take root. If you want to order a bunch of little trees, you usually have to do this by March and the trees will come in April. Trees can start out the size of your finger. These are called seedlings. You can plant them in paper cups on your windowsill for a couple of weeks if you aren't ready to plant them outside. Seedlings are a good way to plant a lot of trees. Not all of them will survive, so it's good to plant more than one. You can order trees that are a little bigger too. These are called "transplants." These may have a better

# Try This

# TryThis

**Start a Tree-Planting Club!**

Order ten trees for each person in the club. They can each plant their trees somewhere in their yard, schoolyard, or neighborhood (always ask your principal at school or neighbors before planting trees on or near their property). If you have ten members, that's 100 trees you've added to the world!

chance at survival, but are a little more expensive to buy. Some types of trees are easier to grow than others. Evergreens such as white pines do very well being moved or "transplanted" and grow fast. You should know what kinds of trees do well in your area before you order trees to plant. Ask someone at your local nursery.

## Getting Started Planting Trees

When you are ready to plant your trees, pick the right spots for them. Trees grow very tall and spread out. Look at the trees in your neighborhood. See how big they get? Make sure to plant your trees at least ten feet apart and in a place they will get plenty of sun.

- Dig a hole that gives plenty of room for your tree's roots to point down and spread out.
- Loosen the soil all around the hole so the tiny roots can grow quickly.
- Pour some water in the bottom of the hole.
- Set the tree in the hole with the roots down and fill in around it with the dug-up dirt. You can add compost to the soil to help give it a healthy start.
- Water it generously. If it doesn't rain in the next few days, you should water your trees by hand to get them off to a good start.
- Check on your trees often. You can feel good knowing that someday you will sit in the shade of your trees. You have done the earth a kind service.

# Green Travel—Walk There or Bike There

Scientists have worked out that it takes an acre of trees a year to absorb the carbon dioxide of a car driven 8,700 miles. How many trees does your family need to take up the carbon dioxide made from your driving? Ask your parents how many miles they each drive per year. If they don't know you can write down their mileage and check again a week later. Then multiply that by the 52 weeks in a year. The national average is about 12,000 miles per year. That's over an acre of trees per year needed to absorb the carbon dioxide, per car, on the road. That's a lot of trees!

Now that you know how many trees it takes to absorb all the carbon dioxide from driving, it makes sense to drive less. This will also save money on gas. If the place you need to go is not too far from home, try walking. Walking is also good for you. Riding a bike is good, too, for both saving gas and getting exercise. It's also faster than walking. Always follow safety regulations and wear a bicycle helmet when riding. Ride bikes with friends to get to places, but also because it's just fun to ride!

### Getting Together on Rides

If the place you need to go is too far to walk or bike, look into public transportation. If your town has buses or trains, get to know the schedules and see how they might work for you. Ask one of your parents to ride the bus with you to a place you plan to go. See if you are comfortable riding a bus. Try it with a group of friends. It's a lot easier than having your parents find a parking place sometimes.

Another way to save on driving is to collect the errands you have to do and make one trip for all of them. Keep a list of the things that need to be done in town, at the grocery store, or at the mall. Try to drive only once for a whole bunch of errands. Carpooling with friends is another good way to save on driving. But don't keep your driver waiting. Idling engines use a lot of gas!

## Save Water

Though the amount of water on the planet stays roughly the same over time, the amount of clean water grows scarcer every day. This is because waterways are polluted by waste water flowing out of factories, agricultural

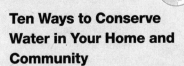

## What Can Be Done

### Ten Ways to Conserve Water in Your Home and Community

1. Install low-flow showerheads, toilets, and washing machines in your home.
2. Fix leaks in faucets and pipes.
3. Turn off your tap while you are brushing your teeth.
4. Only wash full loads of laundry and dishes. A half-empty load uses the same amount of water as a full load.
5. Keep cold water in a pitcher in the fridge, rather than running the tap until it gets cold.
6. Plant trees in your yard and parks that don't need watering.
7. Landscape your home, town, and parks with local species of plants that can survive without watering. Or just make a cool rock garden!
8. Choose drought-resistant species in case of hotter, drier times.
9. Always collect rainwater to water your gardens.
10. Take a shower instead of a bath; it uses less water.

# TryThis

farm fields, oil refineries, and even just off dirty streets and highways. This polluted runoff gets into lakes and streams, but even worse, it makes its way into underground aquifers. Aquifers, or groundwater, are our most precious source of fresh, clean water. They are always running and collecting more water, and so are a renewable source of water for people all over the world. However, in the last century, arid places in the southwestern United States (and around the world) began irrigating for farming or just to have green grass on lawns and golf courses. They began taking too much groundwater, too fast. Scientists call this "mining the aquifer." When an aquifer doesn't have time to collect more water, the water table drops lower and lower until that aquifer can be lost forever. This is a serious problem in dry places. As more and more people live on the earth, our need for water continues to rise.

## Your Greedy Grass

According to the EPA, every homeowner who has a lawn that is just 100 feet wide by 100 feet long uses 10,000 gallons of water each year to keep it green. The most popular grass planted in America for lawns is Kentucky bluegrass, because it is soft, thick, and green. The only problem is that it needs 35–40 inches of rain every year, even though most places average only about 14 inches or less. This means a lot of clean drinking water is pumped onto these lawns to keep them green. What a waste! Even worse, people often add fertilizer. Homeowners in America put 67 million pounds of chemicals on their lawns every year. That's more pounds of fertilizer than are used by farmers!

Ask your parents to let part of your lawn grow wild with wildflowers and native grasses. They can even put a fence around it like a garden. It's a great way to attract birds and butterflies.

## Don't Trash Your Parks and Beaches

People often litter because they are lazy or can't be bothered to find a garbage can for their trash, but when everyone litters it can have an effect on our environment. In addition to the bad effect ocean trash may have on sea life, it often washes up on shore into ugly messes on our beaches and shorelines. Litter on land can be just as ugly, as the wind catches paper and plastic and traps it against trees in parks and along fences and hedges. Picking up litter not only gets rid of the ugly mess, it also keeps our pets and wildlife from eating it or being hurt by it. After picking up litter for a while, you'll see how addictive it can be. It feels good to clean up the planet!

### Make a "Never Litter" Pledge

Don't add to the mess. Never litter. Not even a toothpick. After a while you will wonder how you ever dropped litter. You will notice when people litter cigarette butts or paper. It will amaze you to see them toss trash. If you are planning an outing at the park or beach, always bring a trash bag and clean up every speck of trash you make. Never leave anything behind except footprints!

At the end of the day dispose of trash and donate the bag of recyclables to a school group that is collecting bottles for a fundraiser. Feel great about getting exercise, hanging out with friends, and helping the environment!

## Celebrate Earth Day

On April 22, 1970, the United States celebrated the first Earth Day. More than 20 million people took part in all the events, which included parades, and environmental awareness talks and songs. This marked the beginning of the "environmental movement" where people began to become more aware of how we were affecting the earth. The second Earth Day was not celebrated until twenty years later, but this time more than 100 million people worldwide took part. Now people celebrate Earth Day every year on April 22nd.

## What Can Be Done

### Trash Pickup in General

1. Store a garbage bag and gloves in your parent's car so you can pick up trash you see around your neighborhood.
2. Organize a "trash pickup" hike in your neighborhood with friends. Take turns hiking through each of your friends' neighborhoods.
3. Adopt a highway with your family, class, or club. Then do regular litter pickups there.
4. Plan a picnic in the park or on the beach and afterward pick up litter.
5. Take the time to pick up trash. It's worth it to keep your environment clean.

# TryThis

## Organize a Litter Cleanup Hike

Get some friends together and look at a map of your town. Plan where you will hike. Make the first hike about a mile to see how long it takes. Make sure everyone wears clothes that are right for the weather and comfortable shoes. Have everyone bring work gloves and a trash bag. As you walk around town, take turns picking up the litter you see on the street. You can have one person carry a recycling bag and keep the recyclable bottles and cans you find in that.

This year for Earth Day have a party! Use some of the fun activities from this book as party games. Make recycled paper pinwheels. Eat earthworm dirt cups! Ask everyone to bring a can of food to donate to the local food pantry. For party favors send everyone home with a tree seedling in a cup to plant in their yard. Saving the earth can be fun, too!

## Every Day Should Be Earth Day

Earth Day is one day each year that everyone cherishes the earth. But what if we made every day Earth Day? Start an "Earth Day Every Day" club at school. Make it a lifelong habit—like brushing your teeth!

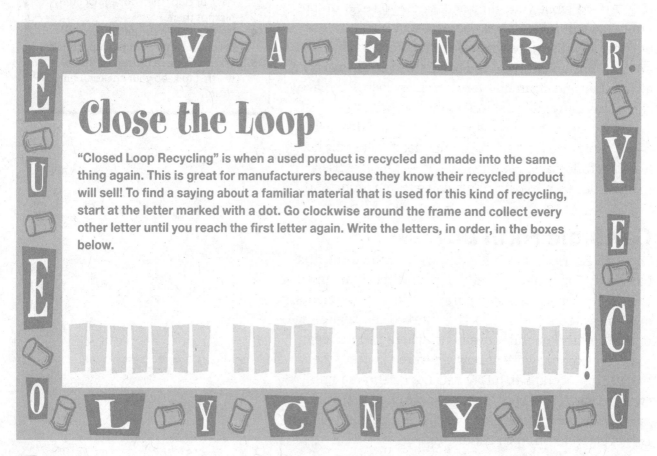

# Close the Loop

"Closed Loop Recycling" is when a used product is recycled and made into the same thing again. This is great for manufacturers because they know their recycled product will sell! To find a saying about a familiar material that is used for this kind of recycling, start at the letter marked with a dot. Go clockwise around the frame and collect every other letter until you reach the first letter again. Write the letters, in order, in the boxes below.

**Chapter 9**

# Actions to Preserve Our Environment

# Waste Less Lunch

Over the course of a school year, even a small school can generate more than a ton (2000 pounds) of food waste from the cafeteria. Imagine if that school also uses disposable cutlery and paper plates! Bringing your lunch from home doesn't help much if most of it ends up in the trash. Use the decoder to replace the symbols with letters and learn how you can waste less at lunch!

A=✿  C=✪  E=✳  F=❋  I=☆  K=❀  O=✸  U=★

T✿❀✳ ✸NLY ✿S M★✪H ✿S

Y✸★ W☆LL ✳✿T.

P✿✪❀ R✳★S✿BL✳ ✪✸NT✿☆N✳RS.

❋☆LL ✿ TH✳RM✸S.

BR☆NG ✿ ✪L✸TH N✿P❀☆N.

US✳ ✿ L★N✪HB✸X.

# We Are All Interconnected

The things you do to help the environment help everyone. It is never a wasted effort to save, recycle, and protect wild places. Air pollution does not respect borders, but blows into other states and countries. Water pollution flows into other aquifers and along other coastlines. Resources can be used up and wasted so that there is not enough for everyone. This includes oil, clean water, and land for planting food. It's important to respect the earth for everyone's sake.

Luckily, there is a lot of information about how to be green and help the environment. You can find most of it online. The Internet is another way that we are all connected throughout the world. It's a great way to get the word out about how to help and also learn new things you can do!

## Cool Green Web Sites

There are many cool sites online that you can check regularly for green tips. This can help you and your family to stay informed about the good things going on out there! Always check with your parents to make sure sites are trustworthy. Here are a few cool Web sites to check out:

- "The Green Guide," put out by the National Geographic Society, gives weekly tips about staying green. Their mission is to "inspire people to care about the planet." You can find them at *www .thegreenguide.com*.
- The Environmental Protection Agency (EPA) Web site tells you about ways you can be safe while protecting the environment. *www .epa.com*
- Campaign Earth gives tips on how you can live a greener lifestyle. *www.campaignearth.org*

# TryThis

### Recycling for Trees!

Start a bottle drive to raise money to buy trees to plant on your school grounds. Make up a flier to put up around school and town about it. This has a double advantage. You recycle bottles and cans and you plant new trees!

# The Answer Is "Worms"!

What is the question? To find out, use the directions to cross out words from the grid. Read the remaining words from left to right and top to bottom!

Cross out words that...
...rhyme with TRASH
...have double vowels
...mean BIG

| CLASH | MASSIVE | WHAT |
|---|---|---|
| SMALL | WOOD | HUGE |
| BOOK | WIGGLY | ENORMOUS |
| CREATURES | CAN | SKIING |
| SMASH | HELP | TURN |
| VEGGIE | VACUUM | WASTE |
| GASH | INTO | DASH |
| PRECIOUS | COLOSSAL | COMPOST |

For more, check out the list at the end of the book, in the Resources section.

## Activities to Do in School

School is a great place to get other kids involved in green living. Ask your teacher if your class will study the environment in science this year and if you can do some green projects when they relate to what you are learning. Even when your class is studying habitats, like rainforests, you can start talking about green topics. Share some of the activities and fun facts you learned in this book with your class. Plan some green projects that your school can do on Earth Day.

### Start Paper Recycling at School

Schools use tons of paper. It is a good place to save a lot of paper...and trees! Talk to your teacher about your recycling idea. If your teacher likes the idea, you can have everyone in your class who wants to bring in a cardboard box with the top flaps cut off. Decorate the boxes by drawing colorful trees, flowers, mountains, and lakes. Then write in big letters, "Save Trees—Recycle!" Deliver them around the school to the classes who want them. Collect ten cool facts about trees to give out with your recycling boxes to get people motivated. You can start with the ones found in this book! Start a contest to see which class can recycle the most paper. This might motivate kids to help out. Give out baby trees as prizes!

### Be Proud to Be a Green School

Talk to your principal about your school becoming a "Green School." There are many advantages to becoming a Green School, like improving learning about the environment through hands-on activities to make the school more energy efficient. It can also save the school money by reducing energy costs. You can get information about becoming a Green School from the Alliance to Save Energy at *www.ase.org*.

### Using School Grounds to Learn about Nature

Many schools have wetlands on their properties, even if it is just a small wet area with cattails. There can be some interesting life cycles going on there. Ask your teacher if your class can go out to look around on school grounds for signs of animals (or plants) in the spring and see what's there. You might find some interesting things! Go to the EPA site and learn about how your class can participate in the "Adopt-a-Wetland" program at *www.epa.gov/region4/water/wetlands/education/adopt.html*.

### Combining Community Service with Green Activities

Talk to your teacher about having your class "adopt" a roadway or park to keep clean. It is a great way to take part in community service while picking up litter! Once your class does it, maybe other classes will want to adopt a road to keep clean too. Contact your county Department of Transportation for guidelines about adopting a roadway to keep clean.

Or you could have a "Protect the Environment" poster contest at school to raise awareness about pollution issues. Give organic chocolate as the prize.

## Getting Your Parents, Friends, and Siblings Involved

Parents are busy. If you can help make green issues easier for them, they might be happier to get green! Get your sisters and brothers involved, too. Here are some things you can do to get your parents, friends, and siblings to help the environment.

**What Can Be Done**

Write to the companies that make your favorite foods and ask them to switch to recyclable containers. Consumers do have power!

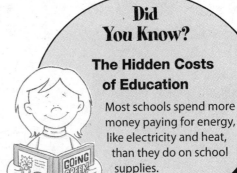

**Did You Know?**

**The Hidden Costs of Education**

Most schools spend more money paying for energy, like electricity and heat, than they do on school supplies.

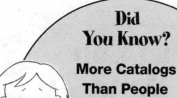
- Ask your parents to shop online. It saves gas and time from driving to the store. Remind them that when they order they have to ask NOT to receive a printed catalog with their purchase.
- Talk to your parents about making their next car an energy-efficient or hybrid car. Hybrid cars get two to three times the mileage of most cars and they are quiet, so they don't add to noise pollution. They will also save your parents money on gas.
- The next time they need stamps, ask your parents to buy federal duck stamps from your local post office. These stamps support wetlands.
- Get your parents to thaw the meat for dinner by taking it out the night before and setting it in the fridge. This saves water by not thawing in the sink and energy by not thawing in the microwave.
- Talk to your parents about renewable energy. Maybe they would be interested in getting a windmill or solar panel. You never know unless you ask!
- Adopt your next pet from an animal shelter.
- Take an ecological vacation. Instead of flying somewhere and staying in a hotel, go camping or hiking to a local wilderness area. It's fun and healthy and will cost a lot less than a cruise!

## Catalog Catastrophe

Though recycling is good, not all states have great recycling programs, so it's good to reduce how much junk mail you get in the first place. Here are a few things you and your parents can do to help. To stop getting junk catalogs, make a pile of all your unwanted catalogs and ask your parents to take a few minutes every week and call the toll-free numbers on each one and ask that their names (on the mailing label) be removed from the company's mailing list. You can also send a note to the Direct Mail Association. For $1, they will remove your names from their national database for five years. Make sure you give them everyone's name in your family who gets junk mail, spelled in every way you get them on labels (they are often misspelled). Send your letter to: DMA Mail Preference Service, P.O. Box 643, Carmel, NY 10512. You can read more about this at: *www.DMA Consumers.org.*

Before you recycle your junk catalogs, make sure your recycling center takes them. If they do, recycle them with your glossy magazines. If they don't, find a second home for them. Keep them out of the landfill by asking at school if you can put them in the teacher's lounge, or maybe the art teacher can use them for art projects. Ask your recycling center to start taking them, too. It can't hurt to ask!

## Activities to Do in Your Home

There are many ways you can save energy at home. Some are really simple and you can do them yourself. Others will need help from your parents. Try a few and see how easy it is to act green!

- Turn out lights when you are not using them.
- Ask your parents to get "compact fluorescent lamps" for your lights. They use one-fourth of the electricity of a regular light bulb, burn cooler, and last a lot longer.
- Don't leave the TV on when no one is watching it. Also turn off computers, radios, stereos, electric blankets, and heating pads.
- Ask your parents to turn the heat down just a couple of degrees in the winter and you can wear a sweater. Or you can ask them to use a ceiling fan on less hot days in the summer instead of air conditioning.
- In the winter ask your parents to close the damper in your fireplace when you are not using it. Heat rises and goes right out of your chimney!

### How Much Difference Can One Bulb Make?

If your parents replaced just one regular light bulb in your house with a compact fluorescent lamp, they would save $30 in electricity costs over the life of that bulb. You would also stay cooler in the summer, because these bulbs give off 70 percent less heat.

### Make a Draft Stopper

You can stop heat from getting out under your doors and cold from sneaking in. Get an old pillowcase from your mom and cut it into 6" wide, two-layer thick strips. Sew up both the long sides using small stitches. Then turn it inside out, so your stitches are on the inside. Now fill it with sand (your parents can buy sand from a hobby shop, nursery, or garden store). Sew up the little end. Now you can decorate your draft stopper with fabric paint. Make flowers or rainbows to remind you that summer will be back soon!

- Don't leave the refrigerator door open. Take a quick look and close the door.
- Ask your mom or dad to get solar lights for your outdoor walkways. They are charged by the sun during the day and light your yard electricity-free at night.
- "Detox" your house. If you can see old paint cans in the basement, old pesticide boxes in the garden shed, or old toxic household cleaners under the sink, you can call the landfill and ask when they have toxic waste pickup days. It's better to have them out of the house!
- Ask your parents if you can get cloth napkins to replace the paper napkins you use every day. Or get some for your mom or dad as a gift. It doesn't add much to laundry but it saves a lot of trees! Handkerchiefs save a lot of tissues and make good gifts, too.

## Stop Heating the Outdoors

Has your mom or dad ever told you to close the door in the winter because you were letting all the heat out? It's true that the heat will escape out your open door, but a lot of heat sneaks out of your house through cracks you may not even realize are there! Researchers have found that people lose one-tenth of their heat through little spaces

The EVERYTHING KIDS' Environment Book

they can fix if they know they are there. You can test for heat leaks with your fingertips. Run your fingers around the edges of your windows. Do you feel a cold spot? That window may need a little sealing to block the cold from getting in. Now run your fingers along the bottom of your doors to the outside. Do you feel cold air? That's a common place for cold leaks.

### Spread the Word

Sometimes people don't conserve energy because they don't know how. They also may not know that they can save money by conserving. A cool poster that tells ways to conserve water, energy, gas, and resources might be a fun way to spread green thinking. Make a list of twenty easy ways to save. Ask your mom, dad, or teacher for some bigger (legal

sized) recycled paper. In big, bold letters write your title, "20 Ways to Help Save the Planet and Save Some Money, Too!" Then decorate the rest of the poster with cool colors, drawings, or clipped pictures from magazines of animals or mountain scenes. Always ask permission to hang the poster at school, or in the local food co-op and other local stores.

## Getting Your Neighbors Involved

Your neighborhood may already have many green-minded people in it, but they may not know each other well enough to work together on community green projects. With help from your parents, organize a Neighborhood Cleanup in the spring. When the snow melts and all the

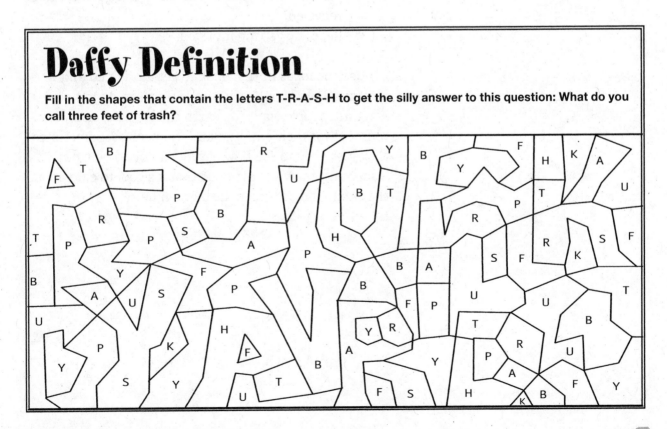

# Daffy Definition

**Fill in the shapes that contain the letters T-R-A-S-H to get the silly answer to this question: What do you call three feet of trash?**

winter litter appears in your neighborhood and park, pick it up. Plant baby trees. Get local stores to donate refreshments. Have a neighborhood yard sale to get rid of old things without taking them to the landfill. You can also help out elderly neighbors by offering to help them recycle. You can get to know all your neighbors and you'll be helping the environment at the same time.

## Hope for the Future

You are important in the fight for the environment, and you can provide hope to future generations. The earth needs your help! Use the four R's:

- Reduce the amount of waste you and your family use.
- Reuse materials.
- Recycle those items you cannot reuse (also make sure you and your parents buy things that can be recycled).
- React by getting involved.

Use the ideas in this book to get motivated and inform others about easy things they can do to help. After all, people want the earth to be a safe, clean environment for their children and themselves. Sometimes they just need to see how easy it can be to help out. Be a leader and show your friends that it's cool to care about the earth and act green. Be a green hero!

# Appendix A

# Glossary

**aquifer:**
Aquifers are places underground through which water flows, like sand, gravel, or even clay. People drill wells hoping to hit an aquifer for a good course of water.

**atmosphere:**
The atmosphere is the pocket of gases surrounding Earth and held in place by gravity.

**benthic zone:**
The benthic zone is the very bottom layer of the ocean.

**biodiversity:**
Biodiversity is how many different kinds of plants and animals there are in one place. The rainforest is famous for its biodiversity because it has so many different species and a lot of them haven't even been discovered yet.

**biofuels:**
Biofuels are fuels made from plants and animals. These fuels are usually used for transportation.

**bioluminescence:**
Bioluminescence is when an animal, like a firefly or deep sea fish, gives off its own light.

**biomass:**
Biomass is the amount of any plant or animal matter that grows and can be used to make energy.

**botanist:**
A botanist is someone who studies plants.

**carnivores:**
Carnivores are meat-eating animals. Carnivores can also refer to the order of mammals that contain bears, wolves, cats, weasels, seals, etc.

**climate change:**
*Climate change* is a term used by scientists to describe a real change from one climatic type to another.

**condensation:**
Condensation is when water vapor cools and changes back into its liquid form.

**Continental Drift Theory:**
Continental Drift Theory is the theory that the continents have drifted apart and are still in motion today.

**decomposers:**
Decomposers are organisms that break down organic matter, like dead animals or plants.

**deforestation:**
Deforestation is when trees are stripped from the forest.

**dodo:**
Dodos were flightless birds that lived on an isolated island off the coast of Africa. When sailors finally found the island in the 1600s, it took only 80 years for the dodo to go completely extinct.

**earth's crust:**
The earth's crust is the outermost layer of the earth, made up of a series of plates.

**ecological footprint:**
An ecological footprint is the amount that each of us affects the earth by using its resources.

**ecotourism:**
Ecotourism is when people visit a place to see the exotic wildlife and natural habitats. Many countries use ecotourism money to help their economy while protecting their natural habitats.

**endangered:**
A species is considered endangered if there are so few of them that they may soon become extinct.

**end-Pleistocene:**
The end-Pleistocene was a prehistoric time some 15,000 years ago at the end of the geologic time period called the Pleistocene, where a large extinction of many large animals took place.

**epipelagic zone:**
The epipelagic zone is the uppermost layer of the ocean where phytoplankton can get sunlight for photosynthesis.

**erg:**
An erg is a big expanse of shifting sand in the Sahara desert.

**estivation:**
Estivation is when an animal goes into a deep sleep through a very hot time.

**evaporation:**
Evaporation is when water, driven by the heat of the sun, changes into vapor and rises into the air.

**extinct:**
A species becomes extinct when the last one of its kind dies.

**fault:**
A fault is where two of Earth's plates slide past each other. This is an area where earthquakes can occur.

**fluorescent lamps:**
Fluorescent lamps are very special light bulbs that burn cooler and use less energy than regular bulbs.

**food web:**
A food web is the interconnecting food chains of who eats whom in a natural habitat.

**fossil record:**
Fossils are the remains of organisms that lived a long time ago, preserved in the rocks. The fossil record shows us when species went extinct relative to the passage of millions of years.

**genes:**
Genes are the smallest unit of heredity. We have more than 20,000 genes that map out all of our traits from eye color to earlobe shape.

**glacier:**
A glacier is a huge mass of ice made from compacted snow that moves very slowly. They are found in mountainous areas or near the earth's frozen poles.

**global warming:**
Global warming is a term used to describe an increase in the earth's temperature from, in part, humans releasing more carbon dioxide into the air. Scientists believe that will lead to climate change with many negative effects to living things on the planet.

**greenhouse effect:**
The greenhouse effect is when gases in the earth's atmosphere trap heat from the sun and build up, raising the temperature of the earth, acting like a greenhouse.

**greenhouse gases:**
Greenhouse gases include water vapor, carbon dioxide, methane, nitrous oxide, and ozone.

**groundwater:**
Groundwater is the water that flows underground filling soil and flowing out into springs and aquifers.

**herbivores:**
Herbivores are plant-eating animals.

**hibernation:**
Hibernation is when an animal spends the cold months of winter in a deep sleep.

**ice pack:**
Ice pack is the thick mass of ice that covers Antarctica, Greenland, and much of the Arctic in winter.

**insectivorous**
Insectivorous plants are plants that trap and digest insects as added food.

**irrigation:**
Irrigation is when man-made water channels are used to bring in water to grow crops.

**keystone species:**
A keystone species is a species that is so interconnected with the other species in its ecosystem that its disappearance changes the balance of the whole ecosystem.

**lithosphere:**
The lithosphere includes the outer part of the earth—the crust and the mantle.

**meteor:**
A meteor is a rock or other matter that enters our atmosphere from space. Its burning passage toward Earth is called a shooting star.

**methane:**
Methane is a flammable gas that is made when organic matter decomposes. It is a greenhouse gas.

**mirage:**
A mirage looks like water in the distance but is actually shimmering light above a superheated desert plain.

**mob of kangaroos:**
A mob is a group of kangaroos.

**oasis:**
An oasis is a fertile spot in the desert where travelers can find water.

**omnivores:**
Omnivores are animals that eat both meat and plant matter.

**order:**
Order is the classification level where animals are grouped between their class and family. The levels start with kingdom and then progress to phylum, class, order, family, genus, and species. A wolf is in the animal kingdom, chordate phylum, mammal class, carnivore order, canine family, *Canis* genus, and *lupus* species.

**ozone-depleting gases:**
Ozone-depleting gases are CFCs, refrigerants, aerosols, solvents, methyl bromide fumigant, and halon.

**monoculture:**
Monoculture is when farmers plant one type of crop only, with no variety.

**nocturnal:**
Nocturnal animals are active at night.

**Pangaea:**
Pangaea was the supercontinent that was made up of all the Earth's continents before they drifted apart 250 million years ago.

**peat:**
Peat develops in wetlands from built-up rotting vegetable matter.

**permafrost:**
Permafrost is the layer of soil just below the surface that stays frozen year-round, mostly in the polar regions of the earth.

**pH:**
Acidity is measured on a pH scale. A pH of 1 is the most acid and a pH of 14 is the most base (or alkaline). Pure water is considered to be neutral. It has a pH of 7. Normal rainwater has a pH of about 6. That is a little acidic because even pure rainwater falls through carbon dioxide in the air. Rain with a pH of less than about 5.3 is considered acid rain. Rain in the northeastern states has a pH between 4 and 5. This is serious acid rain.

**photosynthesis:**
Photosynthesis is the process by which green plants make food from water, carbon dioxide, and the energy of the sun.

**photovoltaics**
Photovoltaics is how the energy from the sun can be made into usable energy like electricity.

**phytoplankton:**
Phytoplankton are tiny, microscopic plants floating on the top layers of the ocean.

**plant transpiration:**
Plant transpiration is when plants open their pores to take in carbon dioxide for photosynthesis and they lose water to evaporation.

**plate tectonics:**
Plate tectonics describes the plate structure of the earth's crust and how these plates move.

**precipitation:**
Precipitation is when water falls from the sky in the form of rain, snow, hail, sleet, or freezing rain.

**producers:**
The producers are at the bottom of the food chain, making their own food through photosynthesis and providing food for all the herbivores (plant-eating animals).

**respiration:**
Respiration is when a living organism takes in oxygen and releases carbon dioxide to make energy to run its body functions.

**satellite:**
Satellites are objects that orbit around another object, like a planet. We use man-made satellites for many technologies on Earth.

**semi-arid:**
*Semi-arid* describes habitats that are very dry, with scrubby plants and hardy animals, but are not considered deserts.

**semiconductor:**
A semiconductor is a material that can carry the electrical charge made by sunlight. Most solar semiconductors are a layer of silicon.

**sky glow:**
Sky glow is the light glow in the night sky over cities. It makes viewing the night sky difficult.

**slash and burn:**
Slash and burn is how some people clear forest for farming. It is when all the trees are cut down and then every thing is set on fire to burn away.

**smog:**
Smog is ground level ozone and particulate matter formed by burning fuels on hot, sunny days.

**space shuttle:**
One of the NASA spacecraft we use to reach Earth's orbit on a regular basis.

**spawn:**
Spawn is another word for fish laying their eggs upstream.

**sublimation:**
Sublimation is when ice evaporates directly into vapor without first melting into the water phase.

**threatened:**
When species are not quite endangered but their numbers are low, they are considered threatened.

**toxic waste:**
Toxic waste is trash that can harm or kill living things, including people. Often chemicals, it can be also medical waste.

**treaty:**
A treaty is a signed agreement between two or more countries.

**ultraviolet light:**
Ultraviolet light is a kind of electromagnetic radiation from the sun that has a wavelength shorter than visible light, so we cannot see it. Though too much ultraviolet light is bad for us, we do need some to be healthy.

**watt:**
A watt is a unit of power and how we measure electricity. A regular light bulb usually uses between 40 and 100 watts of electricity. The 100-watt bulb is brighter and uses more units of power.

**weather:**
Weather is what is going on in the atmosphere at any one time in regards to temperature, moisture, wind, and clouds.

# Resources

## Environmental Groups You Can Join

### The Cousteau Society
870 Greenbriar Circle, Suite 402
Chesapeake, VA 23320
*www.cousteausociety.org*
Educates the public about natural ecosystems.

### Earthwatch
3 Clock Tower Place, Suite 100, Box 75
Maynard, MA 01754
*www.earthwatch.org*
Promotes the conservation of our natural resources and cultural heritage through research, education, and conservation.

### Environmental Defense Fund
1875 Connecticut Ave., NW
Washington, DC 20009
*www.edf.org*
Works to protect clean air, water, and human health. Educates people on endangered species, rainforests, and recycling.

### Friends of the Earth
1025 Vermont Ave., NW, Suite 300
Washington, DC 20005
*www.foe.org*
Defends the environment and champions a healthy and just world.

### Greenpeace, USA
1436 U St., NW
Washington, DC 20009
*www.greenpeaceusa.org*
Works to preserve the earth and the life it supports. It has almost 2 million supporters.

### Keep America Beautiful, Inc.
1010 Washington Boulevard
Stamford, CT 06901
*www.kab.org*
Engages individuals in taking greater responsibility for improving their community environments.

### National Audubon Society
700 Broadway
New York, NY 10003
*www.audubon.org*
Tells people how to use wildlife, land, water, and other natural resources intelligently.

### The National Environmental Trust
1200 18th Street, NW, Fifth Floor
Washington, DC 20036
*www.net.org*
Informs citizens about environmental problems such as global warming, ocean conservation, energy, and clean air.

### National Wildlife Federation
8925 Leesburg Pike
Vienna, VA 22184
*www.nwf.org*
Works to protect nature and wildlife.

### Natural Resources Defense Council
40 West 20th Street
New York, NY 10011
*www.nrdc.org*
An influential lobbying and litigating group on environmental issues.

### The Nature Conservancy
4245 North Fairfax Drive, Suite 100
Arlington, VA 22203-1606
*www.nature.org*
Works to preserve plants and animals by protecting the lands and waters they need to survive.

**Rainforest Alliance**
65 Bleecker Street
New York, NY 10012
🖳 www.rainforest-alliance.org
Works to save tropical rainforests worldwide.

**The Sierra Club**
85 Second Street, Second Floor
San Francisco, CA 94105-3441
🖳 www.sierraclub.org
Works to preserve national parks and wilderness areas.

**Trees for Life**
3006 W. St. Louis
Wichita, KS 67203
🖳 www.treesforlife.org
Helps people in the developing countries plant and care for food-bearing trees.

**World Wildlife Fund**
1250 24th Street, NW
Washington, DC 20037
🖳 www.worldwildlife.org
Dedicated to protecting wildlife and wildlands.

# Web Sites

**The Alliance to Save Energy—Wind Power**
🖳 www.ase.org

**The American Wind Association, Wind Web Tutorial**
🖳 www.eia.doe.gov/kids/energyfacts/sources/renewable/ wind.html#Energy%20from%20the%20Wind

**The CIDA Forestry Advisors Network—Information on Deforestation**
🖳 www.rcfa-cfan.org/english/issues.12.html

**Department of Environmental Quality—Information on Wetlands**
🖳 www.michigan.gov/deq/0,1607,7-135-3313_ 3687-24314--,00.html

**The Department of Health—Information on Noise Pollution**
🖳 www.dh.gov.uk/PolicyAndGuidance/HealthAndSo cialCareTopics/NoisePollution/fs/en

**Energy Information Administration—Information on Solar Power**
🖳 www.eia.doe.gov/kids/energyfacts/sources/renewable/ solar.html

**The Environmental Literacy Council—Information on Environmental Issues**
🖳 www.enviroliteracy.org/article.php/63.html

**The EPA**
Information on Acid Rain
🖳 www.epa.gov/region1/eco/acidrain/index.html
🖳 www.epa.gov/acidrain
Information on Coral Reef Protection
🖳 www.epa.gov/owow/oceans/coral
🖳 www.epa.gov/owow/oceans/debris/index.html
🖳 www.epa.gov/ebtpages/air.html
🖳 www.epa.gov/oilspill/exxon.htm
🖳 www.dep.state.fl.us/coastal/programs/coral/protect.htm
🖳 www.epa.gov/owow/wetlands/vital/nature.html
Information on Endangered Species Act
🖳 www.epa.gov/region5/defs/html/esa.htm
🖳 www.nmfs.noaa.gov/pr/species/esa
🖳 www.fws.gov/endangered/wildlife.html#Species

**The Exploring Nature Educational Resource Web Site**
🖳 www.exploringnature.org

**The Florida Department of Environmental Protection—The Everglades**
🖳 www.dep.state.fl.us/secretary/everglades

**The Food and Agriculture Organization of the United Nations—Information on Water**
🖳 www.fao.org

**"Frankenfoods"—Information on Genetically Engineered Foods**
🖳 www.sciencecases.org/gmfoods/gmfoods.asp

**International Society of Arboriculture—Information on Trees**
✎ www.treesaregood.com/funfacts/funfacts.aspx

**NASA—Information on Climate Change and Volcanoes**
✎ www.nasa.gov/centers/goddard/news/topstory/2003/1023esuice.html
✎ www.geology.sdsu.edu/how_volcanoes_work

**The National Parks Service—Information on the Everglades**
✎ www.nps.gov/ever

**National Recycling Coalition—Information on Recycling**
✎ www.nrc-recycle.org

**The National Weather Service Online School for Weather**
✎ www.srh.noaa.gov/srh/jetstream/atmos/layers.htm

**The Ozone Hole Inc.**
✎ www.solcomhouse.com/iceberg.htm
✎ www.ozonelayer.noaa.gov
✎ www.ozonelayer.noaa.gov/faq/faq.htm

**Information on Rainforests**
✎ http://rainforests.mongabay.com
✎ www.rainforestweb.org

**Smithsonian Institution—Ocean Planet Exhibit**
✎ http://seawifs.gsfc.nasa.gov/OCEAN_PLANET/HTML/peril_overfishing.html

**TreeHugger Ezine—Tips on Recycling**
✎ www.treehugger.com/files/2007/01/how_to_green_your_recycling.php#numbers

**UN Convention to Combat Desertification (UNCCD)**
✎ www.unccd.int/publicinfo/events/mdg.php

**Urban Habitats**
✎ www.urbanhabitats.org

**The USDA National Agricultural Library—Information on Invasive Species**
✎ www.invasivespeciesinfo.gov

**U.S. Department of the Interior, U.S. Geological Survey—Information on the Water Cycle**
✎ http://ga.water.usgs.gov/edu/watercycle.html
✎ http://ga.water.usgs.gov/edu/hyhowworks.html

**World Wildlife Fund—Information on Endangered Species**
✎ www.worldwildlife.org/trade

# Appendix C
# Puzzle Answers

## Chapter 1

### Page 3 • Here It Comes Again

| IT | TAKES | LESS | ENERGY |
|---|---|---|---|

```
IT  TAKES  LESS  ENERGY
TO  MAKE  SOMETHING  FROM
A  RECYCLED  MATERIAL  THAN
TO  MAKE  SOMETHING  NEW
FROM  A  NATURAL  RESOURCE!
```

### Page 6 • Water Warning

CLEAN NEVER DRINK POUR CLEAN CHEMICALS DRINK
LIKE CLEAN PAINT, DRINK PESTICIDES, CLEAN OR
DRINK OIL CLEAN ON DRINK THE CLEAN GROUND.
DRINK RAIN CLEAN CAN DRINK WASH CLEAN THEM
DRINK DOWN CLEAN THE DRINK STORM CLEAN DRAIN
DRINK OR CLEAN THROUGH DRINK THE CLEAN SOIL
CLEAN INTO DRINK THE CLEAN WATER DRINK SUPPLY!

### Page 11 • Great Idea!

Compact fluorescent light bulbs use one-quarter of the electricity that a regular light bulb uses.

## Chapter 2

### Page 16 • Paper Trail

### Page 19 • Recycled Words

1. They hold teeth in your mouth = G U M S
2. They are delicious hard-boiled = E G G S
3. A thin piece of cheese or meat = S L I C E
4. Squares of hard, colored clay = T I L E S
5. Where you go to sleep in a tent = C A M P
6. Liquid from a tree used to make syrup = S A P
7. Fruit with small top and round bottom = P E A R
8. Conceited about your looks = V A I N
9. Look at long and hard = S T A R E
10. Opposite of "push" = P U L L

## Page 21 • **Sign of the Times**

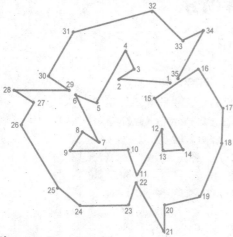

## Chapter 3

## Page 31 • **Historic Garbage**

## Page 35 • **Transform a Tire**

**TODAY MORE THAN 80 PERCENT OF SCRAP TIRES ARE RECYCLED IN SOME WAY!**

## Page 38 • **Reuse That Junk**

Everyone will have different words — here are some examples:

SAIL     PAN
NAIL     PIN
PAIL     SINK
JAR     SAW
PEN     INK
PLANE     SKIS
PLANK     WIPES
JEWELS     JEANS
PUMP

## Page 40 • **What a Racket!**

Jimmy was practicing his violin while his dad was trying to read the paper. When Jimmy would play, the family dog would howl loudly. Finally his dad yelled, "Can't you play a tune that the dog doesn't know?"

The EVERYTHING KIDS' Environment Book

## Chapter 4

### Page 48 • **Message in a Bottle**

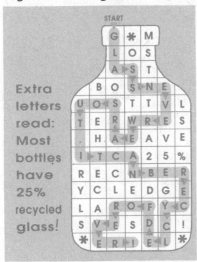

Extra letters read: Most bottles have 25% recycled glass!

### Page 51 • **Much Too Much!**

Teacher: Where is your homework?

Student: I made it into a paper airplane and it got hijacked!

### Page 54 • **Keep the Soap**

MOM: WHAT CAN WE DO TO STOP POLLUTING OUR WATER?

SMELLY KID: HOW ABOUT I STOP TAKING BATHS?

## Chapter 5

### Page 57 • **Close to Home**

SPIDERS
SNAKES
SONGBIRDS
PIGEONS
RACCOONS
FROGS
CATERPILLARS
BUTTERFLIES
MOTHS

### Page 58 • **Modern Motto**

NIOWWD — WINDOW
LUTRTE — TURTLE
TRONH — NORTH
EARK — RAKE
MOWR — WORM
RPLSIPE — SLIPPER
ETW — WET

USE IT UP,
WEAR IT OUT,
MAKE IT DO,
OR DO WITHOUT

### Page 63 • **One Piece at a Time**

T-A-K-E C-A-R-E
O-F T-H-E
E-A-R-T-H.
Y-O-U C-A-N-T
L-I-V-E
W-I-T-H-O-U-T
I-T!

# Chapter 6

## Page 66 • Super Separates!

There can be more than one answer to this puzzle.

PAPER    CANS    BOTTLES

## Page 68 • Garbage into Gold

## Page 75 • Junk into Cash

Evan can sell the following six items to make $4.00: a dinosaur for $1.10, the blocks for $2.00, the teddy bear for 75 cents, and the three cars at 5 cents each. If Evan sells all the stuff at his tag sale, he will be able to buy the bird feeder that costs $13.20.

## Page 76 • 500 Billion Bags!

USE CANVAS BAGS AT THE GROCERY STORE

# Chapter 7

## Page 78 • Powered by the Sun

S U N D A E
S U N K
S U N R O O F
T S U N A M I
S U D D E N
S Q U I N T
D I S C O U N T
S T U N G
R E S T R U N G
S H R U N K

The EVERYTHING KIDS Environment Book

## Page 82 • On the Right Track

| D | R | I | V | E | R | S | | T | R | Y | | | T | O | |
| M | A | K | E | | O | N | L | Y | | R | I | G | H | T | |
| H | A | N | D | | T | U | R | N | S | | S | O | | | |
| T | H | E | Y | | D | O | N | ' | T | | W | A | S | T | E |
| G | A | S | | W | A | I | T | I | N | G | | T | O | | |
| C | R | O | S | S | | T | R | A | F | F | I | C | ! | | |

## Page 86 • Dump Not!

## Chapter 8

## Page 94 • Jar Art

CATCH LIGHTNING BUGS | VASE FOR WILD FLOWERS | STORE LEFTOVERS IN FRIDGE | COLLECT OLD BUTTONS

## Page 96 • Four Fast Fixes

Use both sides of a piece of paper.

Turn off lights when you leave a room.

Put cans in the recycle bin.

Turn off water when brushing teeth.

## Page 102 • Close the Loop

RECYCLE EVERY CAN YOU CAN!

## Chapter 9

## Page 104 • Waste Less Lunch

TAKE ONLY AS MUCH AS YOU WILL EAT.

PACK REUSABLE CONTAINERS.

FILL A THERMOS.

BRING A CLOTH NAPKIN.

USE A LUNCHBOX.

## Page 106 • The Answer Is "Worms"!

| ~~DEATH~~ | ~~MASSIVE~~ | WHAT |
| SMALL | ~~WOOD~~ | ~~HUGE~~ |
| ~~BOOK~~ | WIGGLY | ~~ENORMOUS~~ |
| CREATURES | CAN | ~~SPRING~~ |
| ~~SMASH~~ | HELP | TURN |
| VEGGIE | ~~DREAM~~ | WASTE |
| ~~GASH~~ | INTO | ~~DASH~~ |
| PRECIOUS | ~~COLOSSAL~~ | COMPOST |

## Page 111 • Daffy Definition

A JUNK YARD

The **EVERYTHING KIDS** Environment Book

# THE EVERYTHING® KIDS' ENVIRONMENT BOOK
## TEACHERS' STUDY GUIDE

There are activities throughout the book that demonstrate different aspects of the environment and how it is affected by our actions. Try some activities in class and then discuss their significance and how people can have an impact on preventing some environmental damage.

It can empower students to know they can affect the environment in a positive way. A good way to enhance the educational value of using this book for your Earth and the Environment Unit is by developing, with your students, a ten-step plan to save the planet. It's a guide they can live by for the rest of their lives and share with others.

Following the content of the book, here are some suggested topics to explore and discuss. Look through the book and use this format to choose other issues that interest you and your community even more (i.e., schools in the northeastern United States may want to study acid rain).

### 1. How can we stop rainforest loss?

The Amazon rainforest is disappearing at record rates; much of this is due to ranchers clear cutting forest to provide grazing land to cattle. The beef is sold to fast food restaurants in the United States and other countries. Discuss how people can help stop this (i.e., eating a soy burger instead of beef once a week or more, writing letter to your local fast food chain corporate office, telling others, etc.). **Refer to Chapter 3: Deforestation—The Disappearing Rainforest. Activity: Page 33: Deforestation Frustration—Erosion.**

### 2. How can we have an effect on noise pollution?

Discuss noise pollution and how it might affect wildlife and people. Have half the class listen to you read a paragraph from the noise pollution chapter, while the other half talks loudly. Ask the kids afterward if they could concentrate on what you read over the noise the other kids were making. Discuss how this would affect people in cities trying to sleep and wildlife near airports or roads. Discuss how the kids can help reduce noise pollution in their own lives. **Refer to Chapter 3: Noise Pollution. Activity: Page 36: Noise Pollution and Learning.**

### 3. What is loss of biodiversity and how is it bad?

A simple way to show how biodiversity makes a stable ecosystem is to lay out a tray with ten green olives, ten dill pickle slices, ten celery sticks, and ten chocolate kisses. Have ten students walk by and choose one. When they are done look at what is left. The kisses will be gone—extinct! If one species in an ecosystem is wiped out by a virus, fungus, or a high population of predators, there are still many other species to maintain the health of the ecosystem. What if there had been just one species? It would be gone and the ecosystem would collapse. Biodiversity helps guard against that. Discuss how monoculture farms (big corn fields) can have a similar problem. Discuss how the kids can join a conservation group like the Nature Conservancy to help protect biodiversity throughout the world. **Refer to Chapter 5: Loss of Biodiversity. Activity: Page 64: Make Your Own Plant Guide.**

**4. How can recycling save resources?**

Discuss how reusing things like aluminum, glass, and paper can save trees and power, and lower pollution. Discuss starting recycling in school and at home.

**Refer to Chapter 6: Garbage and Recycling. Activity: Page 71: Make Your Own Cool Art Paper Using Recycled Paper Grocery Bags.**

**5. How can you save energy in your life?**

Discuss small things that you each can do to cut back on energy used in your home and school, such as turning off lights when you are not in the room, getting lower watt light bulbs, turning down the heat (with parents' permission), and more.

**Refer to Chapter 7: The High Cost of Energy. Activity: Page 73: What Can Be Done to Make Less Trash?**

**6. How does planting trees help the environment?**

Discuss how trees help a community by providing habitat for animals, shade, soil stability, and oxygen. Talk about using baby trees as party favors, or having a tree planting party or project.

**Refer to Chapter 8: Planting Trees. Activity: Page 98: Start a Tree-Planting Club!**

**7. What can you do at home?**

Discuss how your students' families can live green and save energy around their houses and yards. Talk about how every little bit helps!

**Refer to Chapter 8: How You Can Help Your Family Be Green. Activity: Page 93: Design Your Ideal Green House.**

**8. How do people waste water?**

Our world's clean water supply is shrinking every year. Think about how people use water and make a list of all the ways they waste clean water. In class, discuss the ways people can save water (i.e., not running the water while they brush their teeth, etc.). Also discuss how the students can get their parents to help, like planting shrubs that don't use more water than is provided naturally by the rain and collecting rainwater to plant their gardens.

**Refer to Chapter 8: Save Water. Activity: Page 99: Ten Ways to Conserve Water in Your Home and Community.**

**9. How can you keep parks, beaches and oceans clean?**

Discuss how people littering adds up. Talk about how you should never leave more than footprints wherever you go. Talk about how pollution, like plastic bags, can kill ocean animals. Suggest ways to decrease the use of plastic bags, like using canvas bags for shopping at the grocery store.

**Refer to Chapter 8: Don't Trash Your Parks and Beaches. Activity: Page 101: Organize a Litter Cleanup Hike.**

**10. How can we spread the word about environmentalism to others?**

Have an Earth Day celebration at your school! Discuss ways to share information that would be fun and informative to others in your school and community. Have students make a poster with all ten of their steps. They can hang it in their kitchen to share it with their family. Spreading green information is an important part of making the world a greener place.

**Refer to Chapter 9. Actions to Preserve Our Environment. Activity: Page 105: Recycling for Trees!**

# Index

The EVERYTHING KIDS' Environment Book

# The Everything®  Series!

Packed with tons of information, activities, and puzzles, the Everything® Kids' books are perennial bestsellers that keep kids active and engaged.

Each book is two-color, 8" x 9¼", and 144 pages.

The Everything® Kids' Fairies Book
1-59869-394-8, $7.95

The Everything® Kids' Magical Science Experiments Book
1-59869-426-X, $7.95

The Everything® Kids' Environment Book
1-59869-670-X, $7.95

The Everything® Kids' Racecars Puzzle and Activity Book
1-59869-243-7, $7.95

The Everything® Kids' Spies Puzzle and Activity Book
1-59869-409-X, $7.95